ADVANCED

MW00749585

I have known Giulio Lorefice Gabeli for many years now and am personally acquainted with his journey of discovery regarding Jewish roots. This book represents a thoughtful attempt on his part to render more understandable the Jewish roots of Christianity and present them in a manner that will not only engage non-Jewish readers, but stimulate them to explore this subject further and implement in their practice some of the treasures they discover there. Read this book carefully, thoughtfully, and above all, enjoy.

—Rabbi Michael Gertsman
Poriya Ilit, Israel

...This insightful book beautifully weaves together the Word of God, history, biblical Judaism, and the personal journey of Giulio Lorefice Gabeli, a man with a passion for God and His Word and a love for the covenant land and the covenant people of Israel.

—Annie Elliott
Director, For Zion's Sake

...As one who regularly encounters people seeking these answers, I can thoroughly recommend Pastor Guilio's book, and I can assure you that you will be enlightened as you take the time to study the material presented.

—David Silver
Out of Zion Ministries, Mt. Carmel, Israel

This book will give you a greater understanding of the privilege of being in covenant with the God of Abraham, Isaac, Jacob, and His family forever... Now through this book we can go on a journey of correlating biblical Judaism in a Gentile context resulting in a greater faith in Jesus Christ who remains forever the son of David and the son of Abraham.

—Dr. Pat Francis
Kingdom Covenant Network

Grafted In, by Rev. Giulio Gabeli, is a treasure chest of scriptural understanding, practical teaching, and spirit-filled revelation... Anyone who reads these words will be enriched and deepened in their understanding of God's heart for His chosen people Israel, and His call to the Church in this hour. Thank you, Rev. Giulio. This is a wonderful literary gift to the Body of Christ.

—Faytene Grasseschi
Author and Director of The CRY Movement and MY Canada

What an excellent opportunity to find a book that endeavours to explain and illustrate biblical truths relating to this crucial topic relevant for the Church and our time. Pastor Giulio profoundly outlined God's counsel from the Scriptures—line upon line, precept upon precept.

—Reverend Aldrin Navo
General Supervising Pastor, Jesus Rock of Ages Ministries (JRAM)

...*Grafted In* is an insightful, fascinating read which also explores the theological basis of support for the State of Israel. It effectively chronicles Old Testament stories of Judaic feasts and observances while also referencing comparative New Testament verses that correlate in symbolism. Gabeli laudably contends with any notions of replacement theology and makes a compelling case for Christianity to embrace its Jewish origins.

—Christine Williams
Public Affairs/Media Consultant for International Christian Embassy in Jerusalem

Pastor Gabeli has combined his years of understanding and experience with the Church and Israel to bring precious scriptural insights about what the Apostle Paul referred to as a mystery. With the battle for Jerusalem and the Middle East as front page news, this book is an important resource for Christians to discern our Jewish roots and celebrate the biblical feasts of the Lord. Good reading for these last days!

—Pastor David Carson
Director, Intercessors For Canada

I am so grateful for the call of God on the life and ministry of Pastor Giulio Gabeli... Giulio's love for God and for the people of the Bible radiates from every page. His profound spiritual insight and ability to clearly present biblical truths will be a blessing to readers.

—Reverend David Distaulo
General Superintendent, Canadian Assemblies of God

For too long, the church has been robbed of her birthright, her Jewish heritage. I am so thankful for this book. It brings a tremendous level of revelation and meaning to the Hebrew roots of our faith. Moreover, it brings a deeper understanding of who Jesus was in the context of His upbringing and culture. Every believer should read this book to discover the hidden treasures of our beautiful Jewish heritage.

—Reverend Giuseppe Platania
Founder and President, The Israel Cornerstone Foundation, Jerusalem, Israel

...*Grafted In* provides an informed guide to engage well-meaning Gentile believers, in a mature and balanced way, in the doctrinal and practical understanding of the Judeo-Christian values of the Word of God. It explains how to bridge the distrust and abuse that have plagued Jewish-Christian relationships. Most of all, Pastor Gabeli will show that it is possible to restore a balanced approach to this subject of Jewish-Christian relations without going off on the tangents and extremes that have, at times, brought reproach to the name of Ye'shua and the Church.

We applaud *Grafted In* and promote its widespread influence.

—Wesley and Stacey Campbell
www.wesleystaceycampbell.com, www.beahero.org

The journey through the biblical feasts, the relationship of Naomi (Jew) and Ruth (Gentile), and God's promises to His covenant people Israel demonstrate not only God's relationship with Israel, but a directive to us, as the Church, to understand physical Israel and the relationship we are called to have today.

—Donna Holbrook
Canadian Executive Director, International Christian Embassy Jerusalem (ICEJ)

Here is a book that will give one a greater insight into the continuity of Scripture and the Hebraic roots of one's faith. It will spark your imagination and encourage you to dig deeper into God's word so that its mysteries, which are self-confessed, will become more understandable and spiritually nourishing. The contents of this book then require a slow, thoughtful read, and those who take time to do it will be richly rewarded.

—Rev. Malcolm Hedding
Former Executive Director of ICEJ Jerusalem, theologian, author, and church planter

From the author's close connection with modern-day Israel and its leaders in Israel as a New Testament Christian, Giulio Gabeli puts into print an interesting overview of Israel—from its calling by God to the present day...

Gabeli challenges all Christians to recognize and remember who they are and where they come from by embracing and supporting the State of Israel, thus bringing honour to the Name of the Lord and affirming the truth of God's Word among nations.

—Rev. Daniel Ippolito
Former General Superintendent, Canadian Assemblies of God

[This] book is very special in that it is faithful to Christianity and New Testament teachings, but it also provides insights for Christians to understand the Judaic roots of Christianity.

Hopefully this book will help bring Christians closer to their Jewish brethren—branches grafted into the roots.

—Avi Lipkin
Author, Political Analyst and Speaker, Jerusalem, Israel

Giulio Gabeli is a long time friend of Israel, and at the same time holds the Church in proper proportion to God's continued plan of grace amongst his people. The book offers an in-depth understanding of truth as to God's dealing with his people, the Jews... Giulio Gabelli has done a masterful job of explaining God's plan and the foundation upon which it stands.

—Dr. George D.Johnson
Harvest City Church, Vancouver, B.C.

Grafted In brings fresh insight to the roots that we all share as believers in Ye'shua. These truths provide a gateway to greater understanding of biblical Judaism, and will stir your heart as the scriptures come alive with fresh revelation. You will discover beautiful traditions that are an integral part of our identity as God's children.

Sandra Crawford
Author, *In the Arms of My Beloved – A Journey Through Breast Cancer*

Grafted In

A Jewish-Christian Perspective

Giulio Lorefice Gabeli

Printed in Canada

ISBN: 978-1-4866-1084-6

Word Alive Press
131 Cordite Road, Winnipeg, MB R3W 1S1
www.wordalivepress.ca

MIX
Paper from
responsible sources
FSC® C016245

Cataloguing in Publication may be obtained through Library and Archives Canada

I want to dedicate this book to my wonderful soulmate Lina,
who has been my greatest fan, cheering me on when the pressure to quit was
intense! I'm so blessed to be sharing my life with you.
To my treasured children—Adam, Edina, Jessica, and Deborah—thank you
for your encouragement and support to write this book.
May my grandchildren, beginning with Victoria Giulia, be blessed
because of this work of love that will remain for posterity.
To my sisters—Elisabeth, Esther, and Ruth—thank you
for believing in me and standing with me.
And lastly, to my mom and dad, thank you for your love and encouragement,
modelling for me how to love my children and believe that
all things are possible with God!

Table of Contents

Acknowledgments

A SPECIAL THANK YOU TO SANDRA CRAWFORD, FOR YOUR encouragement and help in the early stages of writing this book. Thank you, Arezu Papeg, for your contribution and help. Both of you are a great blessing to us.

And to my adopted older brother, Rabbi Michael Gertsman, your wisdom and encouragement to me is priceless. Thank you for being there for me.

Foreword

THE APOSTLE SHA'UL (PAUL) DECLARES VERY CLEARLY IN ROMANS
11:12–19 that Gentile believers have been grafted into God's
ultimate plan of redemption with Israel.

*Now if their fall is riches for the world, and their failure
riches for the Gentiles, how much more their fullness!
For I speak to you Gentiles; inasmuch as I am an apostle
to the Gentiles, I magnify my ministry, if by any means I
may provoke to jealousy those who are my flesh and save
some of them. For if their being cast away is the reconciling
of the world, what will their acceptance be but life from
the dead?*

*For if the firstfruit is holy, the lump is also holy; and
if the root is holy, so are the branches. And if some of
the branches were broken off, and you, being a wild
olive tree, were grafted in among them, and with them
became a partaker of the root and fatness of the olive
tree, do not boast against the branches. But if you do*

> *boast, remember that you do not support the root, but the root supports you.*
>
> *You will say then, "Branches were broken off that I might be* grafted in." (Romans 11:12–19, NKJV, emphasis added)

And thus the title of this book, *Grafted In: A Jewish-Christian Perspective.* The book is the compilation and fruit of many years of the research, and the revelation and restoration of biblical truth in our personal lives, family, and church. What you are going to discover is the answer to the "why" and "how" questions being asked in the global church today regarding the practice and implementation of the Jewish roots of Christianity. I do not claim to have all the answers, or some special corner on God exclusively, but I am confident that my personal journey and experience has afforded me the privilege of writing this book with authority.

My intention is to inform and engage well-meaning Gentile believers, in a mature and balanced way, the doctrinal and practical understanding of the Judeo-Christian values of the Word of God. The obvious challenge before us is how we reverse centuries of ingrained views and tradition that has created two separate camps in the Jewish and Christian worlds. How do we bridge the distrust and abuse that has plagued Jewish-Christian relationships? What does that look like? Herein lies my challenge.

I will attempt to show you that it is possible to restore a balanced approach to this subject without going off on tangents and extremes that, sadly, have brought reproach to the name of Ye'shua and the church.

To pastors and ministry leaders, my heart in writing this book is simply to encourage, empower, enrich, and enable Christian leadership to better understand and truly model an authentic biblical Christianity that will release greater blessing and favor upon the church and the ministries you oversee. All I ask of you is to read this book openly and honestly, removing any filters of negative, abusive experiences with individuals who through ignorance have created damage to the Body of Christ, although they were sincere in their pursuit of implementing biblical truth. I trust that you will appreciate my candidness and transparency.

In closing, I must mention that I will be using Hebrew names and terms interchangeably with the English versions you may be familiar with, quoting from the Complete Jewish Bible and the New King James Version. Having said all that, I welcome you on this journey of rediscovering a viable biblical model that you, your family, and your church can enjoy with significance.

Therefore, get in the saddle and let's begin our adventure together.

—*Rev. Giulio Lorefice Gabeli*

Preface

APPROXIMATELY EIGHT HUNDRED YEARS BEFORE THE BIRTH OF Ye'shua (Jesus), the Messiah, in the little town of Bethlehem in the modern-day West Bank territory, the prophet Yesha Yahu (Isaiah) prophesied under the inspiration of the Holy Spirit that the nation of Israel—the descendants of Abraham, Isaac, and Jacob—would be gathered back to their homeland and rebuild the ancient ruins abandoned through the centuries under the jurisdiction of the Ottoman Turkish Empire and successive rule of the British Empire.

The Jewish Diaspora lasted over two thousand years, but the spiritual climate was changing for European, Middle Eastern, and North African Jewry. Something was stirring in the heart of a people dispersed: a longing, a desire to return to the land of their forefathers, the land of promise given to them by Adonai, the Lord. The covenant that was established, literally cut between God Himself and Avram Avinu (Abraham our Father), was binding, lasting forever. In Genesis 15, HaShem (the Name) or Adonai (El

Elyon, the Lord Most High) appeared to Avram after the slaughter of the kings who had captured Lot and his family. Consider his encounter with Malki-Tzedek, the priest of Shalem (Jerusalem), whose name literally means "my king is righteousness." Malki-Tzedek blessed and assured him that God would surely bless him, and in response he received a tithe from Avram. Shortly after this, God declares to Avram in Genesis 15:1, *"Do not be afraid, Abram. I am your shield, your exceedingly great reward"* (NKJV).

Now, imagine what was going through Avram's heart and mind after that great victory. Would his enemies seek vengeance upon Avram and his family? Logistically speaking, Avram was living like a Bedouin, out in the open, under tents. There were no city walls or fortifications to protect him and his people from the attack of his enemies, so from a human perspective he was in a volatile, precarious situation. It is evident from the text that Avram was afraid—or, more diplomatically, very concerned!

In this atmosphere, the Lord appears to reassure Avram that he is not alone. God makes a covenant with Avram to confirm his promise of an heir and a land that would belong to his descendants. The Scriptures say that Avram prepared the animal sacrifices: *"He brought him all these, cut the animals in two and placed the pieces opposite each other"* (Genesis 15:10, CJB). It then says,

> *And it came to pass, when the sun went down and it was dark, that behold, there appeared a smoking oven and a*

burning torch that passed between those pieces. On the same day the Lord made a covenant with Abram, saying: "To your descendants I have given this land, from the river of Egypt to the great river, the River Euphrates…" (Genesis 15:17–18, NKJV)

Fast-tracking through the centuries of a displaced people, the prophet Yesha Yahu (Isaiah) declares,

"Enlarge the place of your tent, and let them stretch out the curtains of your dwellings; do not spare; lengthen your cords, and strengthen your stakes. For you shall expand to the right and to the left, and your descendants will inherit the nations, and make the desolate cities inhabited. Do not fear, for you will not be ashamed; neither be disgraced, for you will not be put to shame; for you will forget the shame of your youth, and will not remember the reproach of your widowhood anymore. For your Maker is your husband, the Lord of hosts is His name; and your Redeemer is the Holy One of Israel; He is called the God of the whole earth. For the Lord has called you like a woman forsaken and grieved in spirit, like a youthful wife when you were refused," says your God. For a mere moment I have forsaken you, but with great mercies I will gather you. With a little wrath I hid My face from you for a moment; but with everlasting kindness I will have mercy on you," says the Lord, your Redeemer. For this is like the waters of Noah to Me; for

as I have sworn that the waters of Noah would no longer cover the earth, so have I sworn that I would not be angry with you, nor rebuke you. For the mountains shall depart and the hills be removed, but My kindness shall not depart from you, nor shall My covenant of peace be removed," says the Lord, who has mercy on you. (Isaiah 54:2–10, NKJV)

Isaiah prophesied of a time when God Himself would call back the physical descendants of Abraham from the diaspora, like a wife abandoned and grief-stricken.

God's covenant to Avram was fulfilled and satisfied on May 14, 1948, at approximately 4:00 p.m., with 250 guests present to witness the Declaration of Statehood in the main hall of the Tel Aviv Museum (Independence Hall). As the Prime Minister and Minister of Defense of the newly created provisional government, David Ben-Gurion made the declaration of statehood. For the first time in thousands of years, the Hatikvah (the Jewish anthem, which literally translates as "the hope") was sung and a miracle was birthed. The prophetic clock began to tick again, and God's end-time plan was in full-motion.

Right from the beginning of this book, I would like to make a very clear statement to serve as the underlining theme of this book: Israel is the centerpiece of God's end-time prophetic plan. Therefore, we do not espouse any teaching that replaces physical Israel with the spiritual concept of the church.

Biblical Christianity vs. Biblical Judaism

In the following chapters, I will consider with you the biblical distinctions and roles that Scripture assigns to the church and Israel. I will seek to qualify our convictions through Scripture so as to firmly establish that biblical Christianity finds its roots in biblical Judaism.

You may have noticed that I am identifying these two labels—biblical Christianity and biblical Judaism—for a purpose. We must be very precise with our terms because of the great misunderstanding and ignorance that exists within the global church. This confusion has come because we do not define our terms clearly, thus leaving room for error. I remember as a young man hearing one of my mentors, Pastor Daniel Ippolito, teach me, "Say what you mean and mean what you say." I will never forget that coined phrase. It has helped me through the years to communicate my thoughts very clearly.

Now let's clarify our terms. Biblical Christianity is not "Christendom" or the institutionalized church structure that bases its foundation on tradition, dogma, and liturgy. Neither does it strictly represent doctrinal beliefs. In fact, for the record, our only authority for belief and practice is the infallible Word of God: the Scriptures.

Biblical Judaism is not rabbinical Judaism, and there is a vast difference between the two. Rabbinical Judaism is the compilation and practice of the writings of Jewish sages through history who sought to establish Halacha, Jewish law that governs the belief system and daily functions of observant Jews. Though we may consider these writings to be helpful and interesting, they do not constitute the authority for practice in godliness and biblical accuracy. Therefore, we must be very clear in what we say, because it is in this very principle that we find great abuse and confusion in well-meaning believers who go off on tangents and extremes in their desire to pursue an understanding of the Jewish roots of our faith.

For this very reason, I was prompted by the Holy Spirit to write a book addressing this important subject. How does a Gentile church embrace and collate biblical Judaism in a vibrant and meaningful way? What does it look like? How do we maintain a mature balance that edifies and strengthens the church without bringing reproach to the church? These are the questions we will endeavor to answer in the following chapters. I hope you will enjoy this journey with me as I share revelation, insight, and personal experiences that I believe will help every genuine seeker of truth, whether you are a pastor, politician, businessman, or student. So let's begin!

1

History Does Matter

BEFORE ADDRESSING THE VERY ISSUES THAT ARE CENTRAL TO our journey, I believe it is in order that I share with you my personal journey on this quest for enlightenment.

It has become abundantly clear to me that our identities and personal histories play a key role in ultimately discovering one's purpose and destiny in life. It is not by chance or freak accident that one is born to specific parents of a certain nationality or country. God, the Creator of life, has designed us to be who we are. The Bible declares in Psalms 139:13–14,

> *For You formed my inward parts; You covered me in my mother's womb. I will praise you, for I am fearfully and wonderfully made; marvelous are Your works, and that my soul knows very well.* (NKJV)

This scripture very clearly endorses that:

1. God is the giver of life; He is the Creator, not our parents.

2. Every person's existence has been authorized by divine will.

3. If our creation was authorized by the Creator, it very simply means that a human being has innate value.

4. Our value is determined by the Creator's declaration of authenticity.

Intrinsic to this discussion is the understanding of man (Adam), who was created in the image of the Creator. Genesis 1:27 clearly says that God *"made man in His own image... male and female He created them"* (NKJV). This powerful scripture conveys the intrinsic value of every human being. During the process of creation, Elohim spoke into existence the sun, the moon, the stars, the birds of the air, the animal kingdom, the fish of the sea, and every kind of tree, plant, and seed becoming vegetation on the land.

However, His final and complete creation was not spoken into existence; it was formed by His hands. Why is this so significant? All of creation except man followed the same process: HaShem simply spoke it into existence. However, in creating Adam He intentionally formed him with His hands, taking the substance of His creation, earth dust. Man was specifically designed to be God's masterpiece. If you don't see that as God's gauge for what is most valuable, you will have a difficult time understanding HaShem's ultimate plan of redemption.

In Mark 8:36, Ye'shua declared, *"For what will it profit a man if he gains the whole world, and loses his own soul?"*

(NKJV). In other words, "What value do you attach to a soul?" Ye'shua was declaring that one person is worth more than all of creation. Obviously this is diametrically opposed to the views embraced by evolutionists, secularists, and abortionists.

Having established this, let me share with you why our personal history and identity matters. The Scriptures clearly reveal that there are scrolls (books) in heaven written for every living being. Going back to the Psalms, David declares by revelation, *"Your eyes saw my substance, being yet unformed. And in Your book they all were written, the days fashioned for me, when as yet there were none of them"* (Psalm 139:16, NKJV). What a powerful statement revealing that in heaven there are blueprints of predetermined destiny.

Now, I must clarify and qualify this statement, because unfortunately there have been erroneous views, in my opinion, regarding the word "destiny." First of all, I do not believe that destiny is inevitable, that everything that occurs in our lives, good or bad, was determined to occur and that we can do nothing about it. This is a fatalistic view that very subtly embraces a victim mentality. It saddens my heart that many people live under this heavy yoke of oppression, never able to escape the cycle of depression, defeat, and destruction. Surely Jesus did not lie when he said, *"The thief does not come except to steal, and to kill, and to destroy. I have come that they may have life, and that they may have it more abundantly"* (John 10:10, NKJV). Ye'shua has come to reverse the cycle of death and destruction to one of blessing and favor. Over

3

and over again, I have seen families radically change from experiencing the fruit of a curse in their lives to experiencing the fruit of blessing because of Jesus.

I am firmly convinced that our lives and destinies are determined by what I coin "a series of defining moments." Very simply, I'm referring to the decisions we make at critical times in the course of our lives. Consider this: we are not like feathers caught up in the swirl of a breeze, helpless in determining our final destination. Neither can we simply accept, in the strictest sense, the phrase coined in the Hollywood blockbuster movie *Forrest Gump*: "Life is like a box of chocolates. You never know what you're going to get." No, I believe we have innately been given the power of choice, which will directly impact our course and hopefully unfold our destiny.

I use the word *hopefully*, because there are cemeteries filled with the deceased who never succeeded in fulfilling one-tenth of all that was written on their scroll. Often it is because ignorance or wrong decisions crippled them in their lives, causing them to be stuck in a rut of disappointment and disillusionment, and others allowed fear and intimidation to stop them from stepping out of the proverbial box to discover that God has so much more in store for them. Our destinies remain to be discovered, and we can ask the Holy Spirit to reveal what is written down in our book or blueprint.

Consider what the Apostle Paul said in 1 Corinthians 2:9: *"Eye has not seen, nor ear heard, nor have entered into the heart of man the things which God has prepared for those who love*

Him" (NKJV). I used to think this was a reference to heaven and the afterlife, and unintentionally my constant focus was just making it through this life and getting to heaven. But I have come to realize that this verse speaks of our present life and our journey in the Kingdom of God right here on earth. God has prepared awesome adventures and surprises that we can enjoy during the course of our lives. It is clear to me that many do not yet understand what it means to live with exuberance—or abundantly, as Jesus declared.

In fact, I would say that many genuine believers who love the Lord, and are genuinely seeking to live according to His Word, have imprisoned themselves in a religious box, unable to break out of this mindset because they have convinced themselves that their compensation is heaven. Please do not misunderstand me when I speak of heaven in this way. I am not minimizing our joy and the ultimate reward of heaven; I'm simply declaring that we can enjoy a taste of heaven right here on earth. We forget that the earth is our inheritance for now—God created the earth for us to enjoy! Psalms 115:16 declares, *"The heaven, even the heavens, are the Lord's; but the earth He has given to the children of men"* (NKJV). All things were created for our enjoyment, because God is an awesome Father. He so desires to bless us and see our hearts overwhelmed by the beauty He created!

For a moment, let your memory soar through your personal history and experiences. Do you remember the first time you gazed at a beautiful snow-peaked mountain glittering in the rays of the sun, or the vastness of the ocean and the blueness of its water? Have you ever looked upon a valley with its beautiful array of colors bright and vivid, provided for us by the enormous variety of flowers that grow wildly, all placed there by the Creator? I'm sure you can still sense a twinge of excitement and awe. The earth in its original order was created perfect and good and its sole purpose was to be for the enjoyment of the Creator and His masterpiece creation, man.

Even though sin succeeded in marring the beauty and perfect order of creation, God, in His great love, redeemed us and restored to us a hope that is not only reserved for heaven, but is the vehicle that allows us to gaze into all that our Heavenly Father has prepared for us on the earth. Can you imagine the adventures, joys, and fulfillment of longed-for things that await every believer who walks in obedience, pursuing God with all their heart? Wow! The thought gives me a jolt up my spine!

My Personal Journey

I was born on the sunny island of Sicily, considered to be the pearl of the Mediterranean. This island is an ancient land with a long history of invading armies and civilizations and the clashing of the West and the East. Sicily is a desirable possession, affording many seaports and strategic positions. It was the seaport of Europe to the Middle East and Africa and the agricultural delight of the Mediterranean. I was born in the outskirts of the large city of Siracusa, one of the oldest established cities of the ancient world with a 3,200-year history.

The beauty of this land fascinates its visitors and inquisitors, never revealing the centuries of war and bloodshed that has stained it. However, the Sicilian people are very resilient, always believing and hoping for the best, maintaining suspicions and traditions that have helped them overcome the difficulties and occupation of invading armies, always succeeding and surviving the cruelties of their oppressors.

In Siracusa is also found one of the oldest Jewish communities outside of Israel. It dates back to three thousand years ago, when Hebrew merchants crossed the Mediterranean and settled in one of the greatest seaports of the ancient world. In this ancient city, a thriving and influential Jewish community resided. Through the centuries, it continued to flourish despite the eras of persecution, pillaging, and inquisitions—and many times expulsion from their homes and lands. Despite all this, the Sicilian Jews survived and succeeded in reaching pinnacles of influence. Through the arts, many of them became leading musicians, surgeons, poets, artists, sculptors, and refined artisans. Others became the consultants to nobles, dukes, and the aristocracy in general. They served as court Jews. It was the highest honor to serve kings and emperors.

My father's family came through this lineage. My grandfather was a well-known poet who was called upon to recite his poems in the main square to great crowds of people who came to celebrate the annual festivals. Even Benito Mussolini, the dictator of Italy, honored my grandfather, Antonio Giulio Lorefice Gabeli, for the patriotic poems he wrote. Our family, though Jewish in origin, was assimilated into Italian culture. Our identity was hidden and not talked about for years because of the fear of antisemitism.

Fast-tracking to the twenty-first century, here I am walking and living in Canada with a history spanning centuries of culture and assimilation. I fully recognize God's divine intervention in saving my ancestry from annihilation because of hatred and antisemitism. The grace and mercy of God is a staggering thought that many times leaves me in awe. My grandfather and all those preceding him could have been wiped out, and I would not have been born! That thought sends chills up my spine and causes me to step back and declare, "Adonai, you are awesome."

On a side note, during World War II, many European Jews flocked to Italian-controlled territories to be protected from the Nazis and enjoy normal lives with minimal restrictions. The Italians, interestingly, considered antisemitism "the German disease," but for the sake of appearance to their allies, they had in place certain race laws that restricted Jews to certain areas and specific employment. However, they were free to go and do as they pleased as long as they abided by the laws. When Mussolini and his fascist government fell, the Nazis did everything possible to capture, deport, or kill the Jews in Italian territories. In my grandfather's city of Ragusa, the Nazis rounded up ninety Sicilian Jewish men and shot them in the head right there and then. My grandfather was out in the countryside, working near a village called Rossolini, and therefore was spared—once again, the mercy and grace of God. For the record, the Italians themselves saved eighty percent of the Italian Jews from the Holocaust, and this truth is confirmed by the authorities in Yad Vashem, the Holocaust Museum in Jerusalem.

Having said all that, our personal histories do matter because they position us to discover our destiny and purpose. I recognize that my DNA and personal history has afforded me the privilege to speak with authority about what constitutes a viable and effective church model for displaying the beauty of the Judeo-Christian value system and practice.

2

The Mystery: The One New Man

ACROSS THE GLOBAL CHURCH TODAY, THERE ARE A VARIETY OF expressions regarding the "one new man" concept. You will find variations from the ridiculous all the way to the absolute rejection of the value of Jewish roots and practice. My purpose, very simply, is to present a clear and viable understanding of the necessity of communicating the values of the Judeo-Christian church through a balanced approach. My intention is not to find a compromise, for the word itself creates a negative connotation, to pacify extremists or skeptics. I dedicate this book to clearly communicating the truths and values of Scripture, applying them to practical ways that Gentile and Jewish believers can worship together without falling into the two polar extremes of rabbinical Judaism or replacement theology.

What Is the Mystery of the One New Man?

Therefore remember that you, once Gentiles in the flesh—who are called Uncircumcision by what is called the Circumcision made in the flesh by hands—that at that time you were without Christ, being aliens from the commonwealth of Israel and strangers from the covenants of promise, having no hope and without God in the world. But now in Christ Jesus you who once were far off have been brought near by the blood of Christ.

For He Himself is our peace, who has made both one, and has broken down the middle wall of separation, having abolished in His flesh the enmity, that is, the law of commandments contained in ordinances, so as to create in Himself one new man from the two, thus making peace, and that He might reconcile them both to God in one body through the cross, thereby putting to death the enmity. And He came and preached peace to you who were afar off and to those who were near. For through Him we both have access by one Spirit to the Father.

Now, therefore, you are no longer strangers and foreigners, but fellow citizens with the saints and members of the household of God, having been built on the foundation of the apostles and prophets, Jesus Christ Himself being the chief cornerstone, in whom the whole building, being fitted together, grows into a holy temple in the Lord, in whom you also are being built together for a dwelling place of God in the Spirit. (Ephesians 2:11–22, NKJV)

For this reason I, Paul, the prisoner of Christ Jesus for you Gentiles—if indeed you have heard of the dispensation *of the grace of God which was given to me for you, how that by revelation He made known to me the mystery (as I have briefly written already, by which, when you read, you may understand my knowledge in the mystery of Christ), which in other ages was not made known to the sons of men, as it has now been revealed by the Spirit to His holy apostles and prophets: that the Gentiles should be fellow heirs, of the same body, and partakers of His promise in Christ through the gospel, of which I became a minister according to the gift of the grace of God given to me by the effective working of His power.*

To me, who am less than the least of all the saints, this grace was given, that I should preach among the Gentiles the unsearchable riches of Christ, and to make all see what is the fellowship of the mystery, which from the beginning of the ages has been hidden in God who created all things through Jesus Christ; to the intent that now the manifold wisdom of God might be made known by the church to the principalities and powers in the heavenly places, according to the eternal purpose which He accomplished in Christ Jesus our Lord, in whom we have boldness and access with confidence through faith in Him. (Ephesians 3:1–12, NKJV)

In the Apostle Paul's letter to the Ephesian church, he uses specific words to build a convincing argument that the Kingdom of God, in Ye'shua, is made up of both Jews and Gentiles. In essence, our discussion of the one new man is really about the revelation of the Kingdom of God. These two concepts are intertwined and cannot be fully understood apart from each other.

The Apostle Paul uses the word "mystery" a number of times in reference to the one new man. The Complete Jewish Bible translates the word mystery as *"this secret plan"* (Ephesians 3:4, CJB). For example, God has a master plan that will be fulfilled in establishing His Kingdom, and it was kept secret until the right time.

This secret plan, this mystery, was finally revealed in the Scriptures through Ye'shua: the Gentile-believing church would *"no longer [be] strangers and foreigners, but fellow citizens with the saints and members of the household of God..."* (Ephesians 2:19, NKJV)

He further continues his discourse in Ephesians 3, declaring,

> *...how that by revelation He made known to me the mystery (as I have briefly written already, by which, when you read, you may understand my knowledge in the mystery of Christ), which in other ages was not made known to the sons of men, as it has now been revealed by the Spirit to His holy apostles and prophets: that the Gentiles should be fellow heirs, of the same body, and partakers of His promise in Christ through the gospel, of which I became a minister according to the gift of the grace of God given to me by the effective working of His power.* (Ephesians 3:3–7, NKJV)

To me, the least important of all God's Holy people was given this privilege of announcing to the Gentiles the good news of the Messiah's unfathomable riches, and of letting everyone see how this secret plan was going to be worked out. This plan was kept hidden for ages by God, the Creator of everything.

I want to highlight briefly Ephesians 3:6, because I believe it is here where we can understand the DNA of the one new man. Notice that it says that through Ye'shua the Gentile believers were now to become *"joint heirs, a joint body and joint sharers with the Jews in what God has promised"* (CJB). If we rightly understand the significance of these three concepts—joint heirs, joint body, and joint sharers—we will have fully grasped the mystery or secret plan of God through the ages of time.

The Significance of Joint Heirs, Joint Body, and Joint Sharers

The term joint heirs speaks of a common inheritance, and this inheritance is shared by both those who are to inherit. In Genesis 12–15, we discover that the covenant God made with Abraham included land, wealth, and children, which I must add applies to the spiritual descendants of Abraham (the church).

I must take this opportunity to qualify what I mean by the promises of land, wealth, and children. Gentile believers do not have the right of ownership to geopolitical Israel; Israel belongs to the Jewish people. Very simply, to espouse that Gentile believers will receive an inheritance in the physical land is not biblically correct. Quite frankly, the teaching espoused by the Ephraimites, who proclaim that the Gentiles are the new Israel and the rightful owners of the land, is false and completely deceptive.

Consider this for a moment. The issues on the international stage regarding Israel are based upon this very concept: do the Jewish people have a legitimate right of ownership? Biblically, the biological descendants of Abraham, Isaac, and Jacob are the recipients of this promise, not Gentile believers. Let me remind you that our basis of authority is the Word of God, not political correctness or the United Nations. Unfortunately, public opinion and international diplomacy have vilified the State of Israel, claiming that the actions of Israel with the Palestinians are deplorable and resemble Apartheid in South Africa. This sadly has fueled greater animosity in the Arab world, which is looking for justification to hate Israel. Regardless of the political controversy, God's promise and covenant remains secure, and nothing can change that.

I'd like to offer a concluding thought regarding the inheritance that awaits Gentile believers. The Apostle Paul brings confirmation of this by declaring in Galatians 3:16 that Ye'shua is the fulfillment of the promises—or better yet, the recipient. The promises were made to Avraham and to his seed. It doesn't say "and to seeds," as if too many. On the contrary, it speaks of One— *"And to your Seed"* (NKJV)—and this One is the Messiah. It must clearly be understood that if one be in Christ, he or she is a co-heir with Him. Notice what it says in Romans 8:16–17:

The Spirit Himself bears witness with our spirit that we are children of God, and if children, then heirs—heirs of God and joint heirs with Christ… (NKJV)

Gentile believers in Ye'shua become direct inheritors and joint-sharers because they are part of the same body, the same family of the physical Jews. God said to Avraham Avinu, *"And in you all the families of the earth will be blessed"* (Genesis 12:3, NKJV). I believe this joint body, this joint family that is blessed by God, is not a conceptual reality but a quantifiable one. I believe that a mystical DNA is created and imparted to Gentile believers that transforms their bloodlines, which are affected by the curse of sin, to those who carry the generational blessing.

Interestingly, the Apostle Paul continually uses the word "mystery" in his discourse, because there are deep truths that cannot be fully understood by human reasoning or observation. It would seem to me that the one new man DNA is the product of Avraham and Sarah's bloodline, because the Bible says that Isaac would be born through Sarah, not Hagar. Even though we refer to Avraham as our "Avinu" (father), so do the descendants of Ishmael claim the same genealogical ancestry. However, it is the bloodline of Sarah and Avraham that produced Isaac, the son of promise.

Even as the birth of Isaac was miraculous, so is the spiritual birth of believers in Jesus. It's a mystery that cannot be understood in physical, human ways because it is a supernatural event that comes from heaven.

Now consider what the Apostle Paul said in Galatians 4:2–31. It says that Avraham had two sons, one by the slave woman and one by the free woman. The one by the slave woman was born according to the limited capabilities of human beings, but the one by the free woman was born through the miracle-working power of God, fulfilling his promise to make a *midrash* (an allegorical interpretation or application) on these things. The two women are two covenants. One is from Mount Sinai and bears children for slavery; this is Hagar. Hagar is Mount Sinai in Arabia. She corresponds to the present Yerushalayim, for she serves as a slave, along with her children. But the Yerushalayim is free, and she is our Mother. Galatians 4:28–29 says,

Now we, brethren, as Isaac was, are children of promise. But, as he who was born according to the flesh then persecuted him who was born according to the Spirit, even so it is now. (NKJV)

Nevertheless, what does the Tanach (the Old Testament) say?

Cast out the bondwoman and her son, for the son of the bondwoman shall not be heir with the son of the freewoman. (Galatians 4:30, NKJV)

So, we are children not of the slave woman, but of the free woman.

Notice how the apostle uses the parallels to differentiate between Hagar and Sarah. Hagar is described as the slave woman, Mount Sinai, and physical Jerusalem. Sarah is compared to the free woman and to Jerusalem. The heavenly city, Yerushalayim, is compared as well. The earthly is contrasted with the heavenly, the flesh is contrasted with the Spirit, and human capability is contrasted with God's supernatural power. In this portion of Scripture, we can find various applications, but it is more effective to simply focus on the issue of mothers and bloodlines.

The blessing for Gentiles comes through a supernatural, unexplainable, unquantifiable act which allows them to acquire the DNA of Sarah, and just like Isaac become the children of promise. Isaac became the primary seed of Avraham, and the direct inheritor of the promises, because he, in essence, received the blessing of the firstborn son, the One who would carry the generational line and blessing. Thus, the Gentile believer inherits the blessing and favor bestowed upon the Jewish people (Israel) and participates in the ultimate destiny of the one new man.

One final consideration that will bring light to a misunderstood topic is the relationship of Israel and the church in Ephesians 2:19: *"Now, therefore, you are no longer strangers and foreigners, but fellow citizens with the saints and members of the household of God"* (NKJV). Notice that the Apostle Paul spoke of the state of Gentile believers before Christ in Ephesians 2:12 by saying *that at that time you were without Christ, being aliens from the commonwealth of Israel and strangers from the covenants of promise, having no hope and without God in the world.* (NKJV)

Now consider the status of the Gentile believer in Christ Ephesians 2:13: *"But now in Christ Jesus you who once were far off have been brought near by the blood of Christ"* (NKJV). These scriptures make it very clear that Gentile believers have been made one with the family of Israel, and therefore are eligible to also receive the physical promises of blessing and the favor of the Lord in their personal and professional lives. They are no longer strangers and foreigners but fully accepted citizens eligible to receive the rights and privileges available to them. It is as if they were born legitimately with the DNA of the people of Israel, thus the mystery—the secret plan of God to create a family of Jews and Gentiles together, the one new man.

3

The One New Man: What Does He Look Like?

HAVING ESTABLISHED A BIBLICALLY SOUND UNDERSTANDING OF the one new man entity, I need to ask a very simple question: what does that actually look like? It is easy to communicate concepts, ideals, and principles, but it's another thing to flesh them out. This is the challenge before us. It is here that many do not succeed in maintaining an equilibrium that truly honors the Lord.

I have seen over and over again well-meaning Gentile believers who love Israel and the Jewish people fall into an addiction. I call them "Israel junkies," to borrow a term that was first used back in the 60s and 70s to describe heroin addicts. These junkies were so addicted to drugs that they could not function in normal everyday life. They were junkies to society. Now, I know this obviously may be derogatory and offensive to some, but I'm simply using a term that was used by society at that time. The reason I have taken this extreme view is that these very people are so immersed in the topic of Israel—spiritually, geographically, politically, and economically—that nothing and no one else matters. That is neither pleasing to God nor biblically aligned.

Now, why is this extreme? Very simply, this is not God's view! The Bible says, "For God so loved the world." He didn't say, "For God so loved Israel." Israel does play a key role in the fulfillment of God's plan and the ultimate revelation of the Messiah, but the Father's heart is for all nations. He is not willing that any should perish but that all will come to salvation.

Ye'shua came and died a sacrificial death on the cross for the sin of the whole world, and he loves the Goyim (Gentiles) just as much as He loves the Jewish people. Therefore, based on that truth, I believe we can keep the pendulum of what is acceptable and balanced from swinging to extremes. I believe this will ensure that one does not fall into error and thus bring shame and reproach to the Lord.

Once again we ask the question: what does the one new man creation look like? What are the practical elements of worship, structure, and practice? And what do they look like? What are the principles that allow a body of believers to articulate clearly what is effective, and an accurate practice of Judeo-Christian traditions?

In the following chapters, I will endeavor to answer these questions conceptually and practically, giving instructions and examples of how to engage with these truths.

4

Revisiting the Feasts

THE QUESTION OF WHETHER ONE SHOULD CELEBRATE THE FEASTS is really at the center of the Jewish roots issue. Some churches, as I mentioned earlier, very clearly deny the role of Israel and Jewish observances because of a replacement theological view of Scripture. I emphatically reject their view because there is a distinction between the church and Israel; the two, I might add, are on separate eschatological courses, until the end of all things when both Israel and the church will converge to fulfill God's ultimate plan of redemption. However, we must first consider God's timing and calendar to lay a clear foundation.

The *Moadim*, God's Designated Times

On the fourth day of creation, God was designing his divine calendar. His purpose right from the beginning was to reveal to us his plan of redemption through Ye'shua, the Messiah. Obviously, we understand this truth through the lens of the foreknowledge of God.

Then God said, "Let there be lights in the firmament of the heavens to divide the day from the night; and let them be for signs and seasons, and for days and years. (Genesis 1:14, NKJV)

The biblical calendar is a lunar calendar, based on the monthly cycle of a full moon, whereas the Julian/Gregorian (or Babylonian) calendar which the world uses today is based on solar time, the movements of the Sun marking pagan feast days. However, God marks the seasons—or the *moade* or *moadim*, appointed or designated times—and holy days by the moon.

He appointed the moon for seasons [moadim]*; the sun knows its going down.* (Psalm 104:19, NKJV)

In the biblical understanding of marking time, the new moon indicated the beginning of the month and a full moon the ending of the month. In the Hebrew Stone Edition of the Tanach (Old Testament), Genesis 1:14 is translated this way: "And they shall serve as signs and festivals and for days and years." Notice that the word "seasons" is used interchangeably with the word "festivals" to describe how God marks time.

Isn't it amazing that God set these specific times by the lunar calendar even before the creation of any living thing? God does not make mistakes. He calls these periods His designated times.

Speak to the children of Israel, and say to them: "The feasts of the Lord, which you shall proclaim to be holy convocations, these are My feasts… These are the feasts of the Lord, holy convocations which you shall proclaim at their appointed times. (Leviticus 23:2, 4, NKJV)

These are set times to meet with God in a special way as he reminds us of His redemptive plan throughout the course of history. Each feast speaks of Jesus' past, present, and future. Leviticus 23 reveals the template of seven feasts, which are celebrated in two different seasons which correspond to the two agricultural seasons of Israel. The first season for the festival celebrations is spring, and it is associated with the Former Rains. The second is the fall, and it is associated with the Latter Rains, which come just before the harvesting of crops. Now consider the scriptural application and its spiritual significance.

The following verse should be seen in the context of the coming of the Messiah and the redemptive plan of God, which is clearly revealed through the seven feasts identified in Leviticus 23, and its correlation to the seasons of God—the Former Rains and Latter Rains—fulfilling the full cycle of time.

Let us know, let us pursue the knowledge of the Lord. His going forth is established as the morning; He will come to us like the rain, like the latter and the former rain to the earth. (Hosea 6:3, NKJV)

This scripture is powerful, as it encompasses the full scope of the coming of the Messiah and the festival seasons which foreshadow the purpose and function of the Redeemer to fulfill all things.

Now let's identify the individual feasts and their season. The four spring feasts are:

1. Pesach (Passover)
2. Matzot (Unleavened Bread)
3. Bikkurim (First-Fruits)
4. Shavuot (Weeks, Pentecost)

The three fall feasts are:

1. Yom Teruah (Day of Blowing, Trumpets, Rosh Hashanah)
2. Yom Kippur (Day of Atonement)
3. Sukkot (Tabernacles)

There are two feasts that are not mentioned, and they are Chanukah (Festival of Lights) and Purim, commemorating the deliverance of the Jews from evil Haman and complete annihilation.

Notice that the first coming of Ye'Shua is most clearly seen relating to the spring feasts, the Former Rains, and the fall feasts occur during the seventh month (Tishri), which is the time of the Latter Rains. These fall feasts give us insight and revelation regarding the second coming of Jesus.

God's timetable, when understood within the context of the lunar calendar and the celebration of the seven feasts, takes on a prophetic significance that can literally change your spiritual life by allowing you to access heaven's resources while the heavenly portals are open!

> *The secret things belong to the Lord our God, but those things which are revealed belong to us and to our children forever, that we may do all the words of this law.* (Deuteronomy 29:29, NKJV)

Consider what the Apostle Paul wrote to the Thessalonian believers:

> *But concerning the times and seasons [moadim], brethren, you have no need that I should write to you.* (1 Thessalonians 5:1, NKJV)

The Gentile believers of the first century observed these appointed times fully understanding their prophetic significance, preparing them to recognize the timing of God as a blueprint to the culmination of all things.

The sad commentary today is that most Christian ministries and churches are ignorant of the powerful revelation of God's designated timetable and thus are deprived of incredible blessing and breakthroughs in their lives. God is a God of covenant, and once we embrace this view of Scripture it all begins to make sense.

The Dispensational vs. Covenantal View of Scripture

I believe that defining these two approaches to interpreting Scripture is at the heart of this discussion. The view you embrace will determine how you view the place of Israel and the church in God's ultimate plan.

The dispensational view teaches that God has revealed Himself through the history of time during specific eras or seasons. For example, the knowledge of God and who He is was revealed through events, time periods, and key players, be they kings, prophets, apostles, kingdoms, and nations. Very simply, dispensationalism views history from a linear perspective. History is then defined by successive events, eras, and ages. In this understanding, God's revelation of Himself is evolving, and humanity, within the scope of time and space, is trying to figure God out from one generation to the next.

The covenantal view teaches that God has revealed Himself through the covenants that He has established through history. God is a covenantal God who continually reveals His nature and plan through His covenantal relationship with men. Very often these covenants were made with specific individuals who were representative of a people or kingdom. For example, the Scriptures reveal God's revelation of Himself to Adam, Noah, Abraham, Moses, and David, and the New Covenant is revealed in the book Jeremiah. The covenantal view of Scripture sees history in a cyclical way; history repeats itself because God maintains covenant. Therefore, the terms and conditions of covenants are presented in every successive generation, and individuals, nations, and peoples must make a choice to follow through with the terms and conditions or violate them and suffer the consequences.

If you do a thorough research of history, you will discover that God never breaks covenant, but men do. However, God's love, grace, mercy, and compassion always seek to find a man, people, or nation with whom to reestablish His covenant. I personally view Scripture through the covenantal lens, and especially the covenant that God made with Israel, which He will never break.

God's Covenant with Israel

If God is a God of covenants, we must understand that He does not break covenant, or else He would not be God! Consider this thought a little more deeply. If God broke covenant, He would be no different than fallen man; the Creator would be reduced to the level of His creation and He could not be sovereign. Therefore, we can say with certainty that God's covenant with Israel is an eternal covenant that He will not break. The Scriptures declare,

> *For you are a holy people to the Lord your God;*
> *the Lord your God has chosen you to be a people for*
> *Himself, a special treasure above all the peoples on the*
> *face of the earth. The Lord did not set His love on you*
> *nor choose you because you were more in number than*
> *any other people, for you were the least of all peoples; but*

because the Lord loves you, and because He would keep the oath which He swore to your fathers, the Lord has brought you out with a mighty hand, and redeemed you from the house of bondage, from the hand of Pharaoh king of Egypt.

Therefore know that the Lord your God, He is God, the faithful God who keeps covenant and mercy for a thousand generations with those who love Him and keep His commandments. (Deuteronomy 7:6–9, NKJV)

God's Covenant with the Church

I want to draw your attention to the covenant God has made with the church comprised predominately of Gentile believers. The Bible makes it very clear that the Lord will never break His covenant, when He declares, *"I will never fail you or abandon you"* (Hebrews 13:5, CJB).

God is making a declaration that He holds himself to. His Word is firmly established and transcends physical time and space. Jesus declared in Mathew 24:35, *"Heaven and earth will pass away, but My words will by no means pass away"* (NKJV) Therefore, we can trust God's Word, staking our lives on His covenant.

Now, if one believes that God has broken His covenant with the Jewish people, how then can a Gentile believer trust the covenant God has made with the church? As you can see, those who endorse a replacement theological position are questioning the integrity of God's character and His Word. This theological inconsistency has brought confusion and deception into the church and continues to unknowingly promulgate an antisemitic Spirit within Gentile believers.

The Festivals of the Lord

During the forty years of wandering in the desert, the Lord established a template of worship that all of Israel was to observe generation after generation. This template speaks of the Messiah's coming and ultimate outworking of God's plan. However, today we have the advantage of historical hindsight and the revelation of the New Testament to help us clearly identify and define the principle of foreshadowing. This word speaks of symbols and metaphors that were understood and relevant to its usages in the present, but also carry a prophetic future-tense significance and fulfillment.

To rightfully understand the principle of foreshadowing, we must look very closely at the parallel scriptures within the Tanach (Old Testament) and the B'rit Hadashah (New Testament) and then seek to confirm biblical truth with biblical truth.

Rightly Interpreting Scriptures

Too often, interpreters of the Bible create for themselves theological problems and inconsistencies because they take Scripture out of context without confirming it with supporting scriptures. My hermeneutics professor in Bible College would often say, "A text out of context becomes a pretext." It was clearly ingrained in me, as a diligent interpreter of Scripture, that I did not have the license to interpret Scripture flippantly, for this is God's Word and the eternal life of the hearers hang in the balance if we don't follow accurate principles of interpretation.

I was taught to approach the art of biblical interpretation (hermeneutics) just as I would approach the interpretation of any other literature, whether it be a poem, story, or document. These principles of interpretation safe-check accuracy. For example, in school we were to apply the principle of pursuing "the historical grammatical context." We would ask questions of the text like "What were the historical dynamics at the time of writing?" or study certain words that were used, their root meanings, and obviously the contextual significance of the writings.

Another principle that has helped me interpret Scripture with greater accuracy is this: if the sense of scripture makes plain sense, then seek no other sense! This principle has helped me so often in my research and studies because it allows me to apply a litmus test to what I read. I am able to discern very quickly between allegory and symbolism, fact and fiction, literal and figurative. Within this framework, we will approach the topic of the biblical feasts and their observances. I will seek as well to address the implications and their applications for Gentile believers.

Are the Feasts Exclusive?

I would like to begin by stating that the festivals do not belong to the Jewish people; they belong to the Lord! This statement, I am sure, might irritate some people, but the Scriptures make it very clear and leave no doubt that the Lord takes ownership. In Leviticus 23:1–2, Adonai (the Lord) said to Moshe, *Tell the people of Isra'el: 'The designated times of Adonai which you are to proclaim as holy convocations are my designated times'"* (CJB). God has made it very clear that the feasts are designated as special set times in His calendar. The Lord calls them holy convocations, sacred times for God and His people to encounter each other.

I believe that the words "holy convocation" speak of an event so much more significant than a meeting, service, or reunion. There is a serious weight of glory on these holy convocations.

Let's break down these two words. Convocation speaks of "convocating" (gathering, assembling people) with a specific purpose. Throughout history, kings, presidents, prime ministers, and national leaders have had the authority to convocate an army when necessary after having assembled nobles and barons. Only someone who has authority has the right to convocate or initiate a call. In our context, the convocator is God, not an earthly king or president, but the Creator of the universe, Adonai Elohim. Therefore, when you consider who calls for these specific times, it is very clear that these feasts are of the upmost importance. Once again I remind you that God did not relegate these appointed times for the Jewish people only.

Now consider the word holy. What immediately comes to mind is that God is holy. Holiness can be understood in many ways; for example, the absence of sin, or purity in its highest form. The word also carries with it the connotation of being "set apart" or specifically designated for something. "Holiness unto the Lord," which we read a number of times in the Scriptures in reference to the Cohen Gadol (the High Priest), very simply means "separated unto God."

Therefore, by combining the two words, God is calling for a people who will assemble for the specific purpose of being set apart for Him. It is a time of specific teaching and feasting for the purpose of reminding the people or calling to memory God's faithfulness through the course of their history.

The second purpose of the feast was to prophetically declare through foreshadowing God's intended purpose for the future. What amazes me is the greatness of our God, who is beyond the scope of the past, present, and future; God is outside the restrictions of time and therefore is not boxed into history. This allows God to see the big picture of life from its inception to its completion. In other words, God connects all the dots through the course of time. The future evolves from history, and history conceives the future. God sees it all, and therefore He establishes a day, a season, a designated time to fulfill His purposes and plan.

The biblical feasts are times of such great importance that even shifts in the heavens take place without the majority of the worldwide church noticing. I'll now make a provocative statement, but please promise that you will not stone me or call me a heretic. I believe that the biblical feasts contain, encoded in their very DNA, the secrets of God's inner counsel and the unfolding of His ultimate master plan for all of creation! Now, that is a loaded statement that will require quite a bit of cerebral chewing. However, if you will embrace this truth you will have a much better understanding of the continuity of God's plan throughout Old Testament history, climaxing with the second coming of Ye'shua to the earth to establish His millennial reign.

This is obviously the overall picture, the general outlook regarding the observance of the feasts and their spiritual significance, but as you consider the individual feasts and the fine details, you will discover that they are filled with revelation—nuggets of truth that are connected to every doctrinal belief and practice of traditional Christianity. For this reason, I reiterate what I declared at the very beginning: understanding the Jewish roots of Christianity will enrich one's personal spiritual life.

The feasts serve to remind us that God is the sovereign Lord even over time and seasons. As we consider the different feasts, allow the Holy Spirit to illuminate this truth, confirming all the more that Adonai has established these specific encounters with purpose.

5

Pesach (Passover)

IN LEVITICUS 23, ADONAI SPEAKS TO MOSHE, REVEALING TO him the requirements of the designated times and specific instructions to observe them. The very first feast of great importance is celebrated during the first month of the biblical spiritual calendar, Nissan. The observance begins on the eve of the fourteenth day, which is called Erev Pesach. Let me remind you that the biblical understanding of day and night is measured in twelve-hour intervals commencing at 6:00 p.m.

In the observance of this feast in Old Testament times, a lamb was sacrificed and every individual family killed their own lamb and feasted together, remembering God's deliverance from Egyptian bondage and slavery. The bitter herbs were eaten to remind them of the bitterness of hard labor they endured under their slave masters. The shed blood reminded them of the covering over their home that saved the lives of their firstborn children from the angel of death. During this night, families would gather to celebrate and remember the goodness of Adonai Elohim and His faithfulness to His covenant to Avraham Avinu. Following Erev Pesach (the eve of Passover) would commence the observance of seven days of eating matzah, unleavened bread, and the observance of a special holy convocation of worship and prayer focusing on the Lord. The next six days were workdays, but with the observance of eating matzah during meal times until the seventh day, when they would come and worship corporately, followed by a festive meal with their families.

The biblical observance of Pesach is much simpler than the rabbinical observance of the feast. It is important that I remind you that rabbinical Judaism developed through the centuries as traditions and observances that are not recorded in the Scriptures. I am not suggesting that they are wrong, nor am I suggesting that they cannot be helpful in creating an environment of teaching and instruction.

The Passover Seder, as it is called, can truly be a time of great significance and joy for an individual family or church group. It provides an opportunity for learning, fellowship, and family bonding.

There are many wonderful Haggadahs, which literally means "the retelling of the story," or very simply the order of the Passover observance, the Seder that one can purchase and follow. The ceremonial observances can be varied and modified, according to one's cultural background and tradition.

In the Jewish world, there are two specific categories that identify the Jews in the Diaspora—the scattering of the Jewish people after the Romans destroyed Jerusalem and forced them out of their land.

The Diaspora Jews

Generally speaking, there are two main categories of Jews spread out in the Diaspora: the Sephardic and the Ashkenazi. Very simply, the Ashkenazi Jews are identified as the Eastern European and Russian Jews, many of whom speak Yiddish, a German-English mix. The Sephardic Jews are those who originally came from Spain (in Hebrew, Sepharad) and were spread out in Western Europe and around the Mediterranean. The Sephardic or Mediterranean Jews were very often forced through expulsion to leave their countries of birth because of antisemitism and hatred. When you specifically look at the history of the Sephardic Jews, you will discover that this colony of Spanish Jews was one of the earliest settlements, established during the time of Solomon's reign.

In 2 Chronicles 9:21, the Bible records that King Solomon would send out ships to Tar-shish, which would return every three years with gold, silver, ivory, apes, and peacocks. Tar-shish is a region in modern-day Spain. During this time of exploration and discovery, a Jewish colony was established and it thrived for many years. The Scripture mentions Tar-shish, or the ships of Tar-shish, to describe the wealth that would come with the return of these ships. In essence, they were merchant ships. Therefore, the ships of Tar-shish were also used in a metaphoric sense to speak of the abundance and provision of the Lord for those who seek Him.

Consider as well the story of Jonah, which reveals the importance of the colony. In disobedience to God's express command to go to Nineveh, Jonah headed in the opposite direction, towards the Great Sea (the Mediterranean). There he boarded a ship in Jaffa and headed West. The Bible says that he was going to Tar-shish, fleeing from the Lord. We must ask ourselves, why was he going to Tar-shish? The answer is very obvious: there was a Jewish colony there where he knew he could live with his own people!

Through centuries of conquest and exile, this Jewish colony continued to thrive and grow, becoming very numerous in population. It was not until the fourteenth century that the Spanish aristocracy decided to expel the Jewish community during the reign of King Ferdinand and Queen Isabella. The Sephardic Jews fled to all the southern and eastern European nations, as well as to the North African nations, to begin new lives, and thus we have the Sephardic Diaspora. The language of these Jews was Ladino, a kind of Spanish mixture, but they embraced the language and culture of the nation they resided in as well.

During this time, many of these Jews were forced to assimilate into the cultural identity of the nation because of constant persecution and trouble. There were, however, some Jews who chose to maintain Jewish traditions as "crypto Jews," which very simply means Jews with hidden identities, practicing Judaism underground. Their fear of discovery was very real, so they often would not circumcise their boys, lest they be discovered. Such was the plight of these Sephardic Jews.

In the context of the Biblical feasts (the designated times), the Ashkenazi and Sephardic practiced and observed the core elements (mitzvahs, the commands of the Lord), but each one adopted and implemented specific traditions that were native to their cultural expressions. For the church of the Lord Jesus Christ, we must recognize the biblical observance and contrast it with the rabbinical observance of the feast. Once again, I remind you that you can enjoy a Pesach Seder with the centrality of Ye'shua as the fulfillment, and it will enrich the congregation or your family.

In closing this consideration of the feast of Pesach, I suggest two Haggadahs that will be helpful to you. The first one is a Messianic Jewish Haggadah, prepared by Lars Anderson in 2000 and called *The Feast of Passover Haggadah*.[1] As I have mentioned earlier, the word Haggadah, in the strictest sense, means "the telling." This meaning is based upon the scriptural command from the Lord to Israel in Exodus 13:8, which says, *"And you shall tell your son in that day, saying, 'This is done because of what the Lord did for me when I came up from Egypt'"* (NKJV).

The second Haggadah is a more traditional Seder, called *The Passover Haggadah*, which can be found in Jewish bookstores.[2] These two Haggadahs can be purchased and used in the Passover celebration. Gentile believers can enjoy the variations of the different Haggadahs without losing sight of the central theme of Jesus as the Lamb of God.

A final touch to a Pesach Seder is the celebration in which people dance together in a circular motion. The Mecholah,

---

[1] Lars Anderson, *The Feast of Passover Haggadah* (Pensacola, FL: The Watchman International, 2000).

[2] *The Passover Haggadah* (Herzalia, Israel: Palphot, Ltd.).

or the Hora, is a communal dance that can bring so much joy and bonding in a congregation or family with Jewish folk music.

To our Jewish-Italian family, dancing together during times of specific celebrations has been among some of our most cherished and memorable times. Therefore, I encourage you to get up and dance together, holding hands in a circular fashion, young and old proclaiming that you belong to each other. By doing this, you can create your own lasting memories!

6

Shavu'ot (Pentecost)

THE NEXT MAJOR FEAST IS CELEBRATED SEVEN WEEKS AFTER the last day of Pesach (forty-nine days later). The feast of Shavu'ot literally means "weeks." Leviticus 23:15–21 records God's specific instructions for this designated time.

The biblical observance involves the first-fruits of the harvest, which are presented to the Lord. Bikkurim (first-fruits) speaks of Thanksgiving, specifically for the early harvest of wheat. Each family would bring two loaves of challah bread (bread with leaven) and present it to the priest. With great ceremony, the two loaves were waved in every direction before the Lord. This was a public statement of God's provision for all His people.

I personally believe that the two loaves represent the Jew and the Gentile, and the concept of the one new man. There is a reference to the bread in 1 Corinthians 10:

The bread which we break, is it not the communion of the body of Christ? For we, though many, are one

bread and one body; for we all partake of that one bread.
(1 Corinthians 10:16–17, NKJV)

Here we see the metaphor of the loaf of bread representing the body (people), so it is very possible that the two loaves being waved before the Lord represent the harvest of souls, both Jews and Gentiles.

Now consider the correlation of the Feast of Shavu'ot and the outpouring of the Holy Spirit in the fullness of the feast referred to as well as Pentecost, fifty days after Pesach. During this Festival of First-Fruits (or Weeks), the Scripture reading comes from Exodus 19–20, which commemorates the giving of the Law on Mount Sinai; Ezekiel 1, which tells of the prophet's vision of God's glory; and the scroll of Ruth, because it takes place during the spring harvest.

The giving of the Law (Torah) is of the utmost importance, because it's the very thing that distinguishes Israel from the other nations. We are people who were privileged to receive the light of life, a people who were called to be a light to the Gentile world, revealing and reflecting the light of God which would deliver the nations from the bondage of spiritual darkness. This is why many Orthodox Jews, in preparation for Shavu'ot, study the Torah all night: because it is the Word of God.

Ezekiel 1, the second portion of Scripture read, is significant in understanding the revelation of the Holy Spirit's outpouring. If you will compare Acts 2 and Ezekiel 1, you will discover similarities in the visible manifestation of the Holy Spirit's outpouring. Acts 2:2 declares,

And suddenly there came a sound from heaven, as of a rushing mighty wind, and it filled the whole house where they were sitting. (NKJV)

Consider what the prophet Ezekiel saw as the Lord opened his spiritual eyes. He says,

Then I looked, and behold, a whirlwind was coming out of the north, a great cloud with raging fire engulfing itself; and brightness was all around it and radiating out of its midst like the color of amber, out of the midst of the fire. (Ezekiel 1:4, NKJV)

Both eyewitness accounts describe seeing a wind and fire, one describing the glory of the Lord and the other the outpouring of the Ruach Ha Kodesh (the Holy Spirit)—or more accurately, the breath of the Holy One.

Amazingly, the disciples were told by Ye'shua to go and wait in Jerusalem for the coming of the Holy Spirit, but obviously they could not grasp or know what that would look like. However, they could have been reading Ezekiel's account of the glory of God in heaven when they heard the sound and felt the violent wind filling the house and the tongues of fire resting upon their heads. They might have then recognized what was happening.

The sound and sight of heaven overwhelmed them and they began to utter praise, proclaiming in other tongues the greatness of God in heavenly and earthly languages. Both categories of languages were speaking about *"the great things God has done"* (Acts 2:11, CJB). The visible supernatural manifestation of heaven's reality caused a sound to be heard farther than the upper room locale, and I believe that correlates with the principle of first-fruits and the reading of the scroll of Ruth (the Megilloth).

The Bible declares that the sound of the outpouring of the Holy Spirit upon those gathered in the upper room attracted the crowds and gave the apostles an opportunity to proclaim the Gospel. Peter stood up and addressed the crowds, and that day three thousand people were added to the church.

The Story of Ruth

We have already clearly established that the one new man concept addressed by the Apostle Paul in Ephesians 2–3 reveals God's ultimate plan of bringing into oneness Jew and Gentile believers. The story of Ruth, I believe, embodies this concept and remains the most powerful example of what it means to be grafted in for Gentiles. A cursory look at the story will enable us to see the spiritual insights, truths, and parallels. I would encourage you to read the four chapters of Ruth to familiarize yourself with the finer details.

The story begins with a family from Beit Lechem (Bethlehem), which literally means in Hebrew "house of bread." This village was aptly named, because of its abundance of grain and the very fertile soil that was used to grow wheat and barley.

However, a famine struck the area and life became very difficult. The father, Elimelekh, his wife Na'omi, and his two sons, Machlon and Kilyon, decided to leave their home and village and settle in the country of Moab (modern-day Jordan). The two sons, in the course of time, married two Gentile women, Orpah and Ruth.

For a moment, consider this initial parallel. The family was forced to leave their homeland because of a crisis, and thus joined the Diaspora of many Jews throughout the world. While in the Diaspora, their children intermarried, as was very common throughout history, right up until this day.

The Scripture gives us highlights of this family story by simply saying in Ruth 1:4–5 that they lived in Moab ten years before the two sons died. We are not told how or why they died, but that they joined their father Elimelekh, who had died already. Tragedy had touched this family and Na'omi was left with her two daughters-in-law. All three were widows, facing a very grim future. In those days, there were no government-sponsored social programs they could access; a woman's life and welfare was dependent upon her husband or father. They were at a crossroads, seeking to find answers to their questions. They asked, "Why, God?" This reminds me of the constant cry to God throughout history of the Jewish people, who often were subject to antisemitism and hatred. I think of the atrocities committed in Europe and the Middle East during the Crusades, the Spanish Inquisition, the pogroms, the racial laws of 1938, and the Holocaust. Even today, they face a constant threat from the extreme

Islamic world that threatens to destroy the State of Israel and exterminate the Jewish people.

Na'omi's cry was from a deep wound of disillusionment and confusion: *"I feel very bitter that the hand of Adonai has gone out against me"* (Ruth 1:13, CJB). I believe that within the heart of our people there remains a little corner where we nurture this question and all the emotions that go with it. "Why, God? We are supposed to be your chosen people!"

In Na'omi, we see the picture of the Jews in diaspora through the centuries, victims to trouble and tragedy not of their making. But there was a turn of events: Na'omi heard that Elohim had looked with favor upon the land of Israel, which was prospering agriculturally again, and so she decided it was time for Aliyah—in other words, for her to return to her land.

Consider today's parallel: we have witnessed the modern-day miracle of May 14, 1948, at 4:00 p.m., when David Ben Gurion declared that the official State of Israel, and the Jewish people, were legally and democratically entitled to be in their land. The wandering Jew, if he so chose, could return to his land of promise and inheritance, even in the face of hardship and war. Many have done Aliyah to Israel, and presently the Jews in Israel number approximately seven million.

The picture is so prophetic as Naomi announces to her two daughters-in-law that she will go back to Israel and that they must return to their relatives. They began to weep and hold on to her, refusing to let her go; she insisted that she could not provide them with more sons, therefore they should return to their extended families.

The response of Orpah and Ruth is a picture of the Gentile church as a whole in their relationship to Israel. Orpah loved her mother-in-law and was ready to go with her, but when push came to shove, so to speak, she capitulated and retreated to pursue her own security, comfort, and convenience. Many believers and churches today recognize the role and place of Israel—they honor the Jewish people and Israel because of biblical history—but when push comes to shove, they symbolically kiss Israel and abandon her. It is very sad to me that they have the privilege of entering into covenant with the Jewish people, but refuse to maintain their covenant relationship because it is not convenient.

Ruth, on the other hand, refused to leave Na'omi. The Scriptures say, *"But [Ruth] stuck with her"* (Ruth 1:14, CJB). The word used here in the Hebrew is very interesting, because it is the word used to describe the oneness that a husband and wife enter into through the covenant of marriage. In the scroll of B'resheet (Genesis), the Scripture records the details of that first marriage covenant between Adam and Eve. In Genesis 2:21–24, we read,

> *And the Lord God caused a deep sleep to fall on Adam, and he slept; and He took one of his ribs, and closed up the flesh in its place. Then the rib which the Lord God had taken from man He made into a woman, and He brought her to the man.*

And Adam said:

"This is now bone of my bones And flesh of my flesh; She shall be called Woman, Because she was taken out of Man."

Therefore a man shall leave his father and mother and be joined to his wife, and they shall become one flesh.
(NKJV)

It is very clear to me that Ruth's posture should be the posture of every Gentile believer. God's ultimate plan is to bring His Gentile bride into a oneness relationship with the Jewish people. This one new man can only happen through a covenant relationship in Jesus and a willingness to sacrifice to establish a *berith*, a covenant that cannot be broken. The words of this young Gentile widow model covenant love and relationship for the church.

But Ruth said: "Entreat me not to leave you, or to turn back from following after you; for wherever you go, I will go; and wherever you lodge, I will lodge; your people shall be my people, and your God, my God. Where you die, I will die, and there will I be buried. The Lord do so to me, and more also, if anything but death parts you and me."
(Ruth 1:16–17, NKJV)

Na'omi, seeing the determination of Ruth, embraced her and they began their journey together back to Eretz-Isra'el. The picture is truly prophetic: a Gentile woman refused to let go of her Jewish mother-in-law who did not have anything more to offer her. What a display of selfless love, a genuine unconditional love that desired solely to give and not take. A love that could break through any hardness, bitterness, or suspicion. Reaching the Jewish people requires this magnitude of love; nothing else will suffice.

Consider that Christian-Jewish relationships throughout history have been severely strained and Christian credibility is almost non-existent because of antisemitism and hatred of the Jews. Jewish memory goes way back; they will not easily forget the centuries of hatred, abuse, and cruelty perpetrated upon them by those who called themselves Christians or followers of Jesus. We must recognize that reaching the Jewish people requires a determination to reverse centuries of stereotyping and an image of Christianity—or more correctly, Christendom. But it is possible: many Jews today recognize that the Jewish carpenter from Nazareth is the promised Messiah, the Son of David. That, my friends, is exciting!

We can take one final spiritual insight from the scroll of Ruth, apart from the obvious parallel of Boaz and Ye'shua (the Kinsmen Redeemer). It happens in the aftermath of the wedding of Boaz and Ruth. Through this marriage, Boaz declared to the city elders that an heir would be raised up in the name of the deceased. Notice what he says in Ruth 4:10:

Moreover, Ruth the Moabitess, the widow of Mahlon, I have acquired as my wife, to perpetuate the name of the dead through his inheritance, that the name of the dead may not be cut off from among his brethren and from his position at the gate. You are witnesses this day. (NKJV)

Notice the response of the city elders:

The Lord make the woman who is coming to your house like Rachel and Leah, the two who built the house of Israel; and may you prosper in Ephrathah and be famous in Bethlehem. May your house be like the house of Perez, whom Tamar bore to Judah, because of the offspring which the Lord will give you from this young woman. (Ruth 4:11–12, NKJV)

The parallel is so powerful! A Gentile woman being grafted into the generational line of blessing, honored like Rachel and Leah, the matriarchs of the nation. Furthermore, the city elders prophesied about the child that would be born (the seed) and compared this child to Perez, whom Tamar bore to Judah. The significance is unmistakable; the name Perez means "breaking out" or "breakthrough," according to Genesis 38:29.

If you read the entire chapter, you will discover that Tamar was the wife of Judah's deceased firstborn son, Er. The tragedy in this story is that Judah lost two sons, and Tamar was barren. The third son, Shelah, was not of age, but Judah was afraid that he would die as well if he married Tamar. Notice how Tamar deceived Judah to maintain and sustain the family line promised to her; she disguised herself as a prostitute, slept with her father-in-law, and got pregnant. When the news came that Tamar was pregnant, implying an action of immorality, Judah was furious and demanded that she be burned alive.

What then happened is very significant in the context of understanding generational promises and blessing: Tamar presented the signet, the cords, and the staff that identified the father of the seed in her womb. Very simply, when Judah propositioned her, she asked as payment his seal, the cords, and the staff. Judah, obviously very much controlled by his physical passion at the time, foolishly gave a woman he did not know his symbols of authority (his signet and its cords) and identity (his staff). These objects were precious because an individual's lineage (or pedigree) in ancient times was etched on the staff describing his family line. The signet with its cords identified and afforded the bearer the power of attorney, so to speak. Tamar was very strategic in asking for them, because it rightly belonged to her seed, the firstborn of Judah. Thus Perez became the bearer of the firstborn blessing, following the generational line of Judah.

Going back to Ruth and Boaz, they had a son and named him Obed, who became the grandfather of David, from whose line the Meshiach, the Son of David, would come to redeem all things. In Ruth 4:18–22, you will read as an addendum to the scroll a genealogical record beginning with Perez and ending with David. Here we see the parallel of the Gentile church grafted into the lineage of the Messiah's generational line.

Here's a final thought about Naomi in Ruth 4:14–17:

Then the women said to Naomi, "Blessed be the Lord, who has not left you this day without a close relative; and may his name be famous in Israel! And may he be to you a restorer of life and a nourisher of your old age; for your daughter-in-law, who loves you, who is better to you than seven sons, has borne him." Then Naomi took the child and laid him on her bosom, and became a nurse to him. Also the neighbor women gave him a name, saying, "There is a son born to Naomi." And they called his name Obed. He is the father of Jesse, the father of David. (NKJV)

It is so very important to read Scripture and pay close attention to every word, because very often we allow our denominational lens to determine our understanding of what we are reading. Please notice very clearly that the women identified the baby that was born to Ruth as "the redeemer." To repeat, Ruth 4:15–16 says,

And may he be to you a restorer of life and a nourisher of your old age; for your daughter-in-law, who loves you, who is better to you than seven sons, has borne him." Then Naomi took the child and laid him on her bosom, and became a nurse to him. (NKJV)

The latter part of this verse declares that Naomi would nurse the child, and Naomi began to produce milk in her old age. Wow! What a powerful prophetic parallel. When the Gentile church clings to Israel (Naomi) and loves the Bridegroom (Ye'shua), the one new man (Obed) will be birthed to supernaturally bring spiritual life and restoration to Israel in all her weariness and disillusionment. The beauty of this picture is that Israel (Naomi) will provide the milk of the Word to nourish the one new man and be fully restored to her rightful place. The Scriptures declare that from Zion (Jerusalem), the Word of the Lord will go forth. Consider the prophecy in Micah 4:1–2:

> *Now it shall come to pass in the latter days that the mountain of the Lord's house shall be established on the top of the mountains, and shall be exalted above the hills; and peoples shall flow to it. Many nations shall come and say, "Come, and let us go up to the mountain of the Lord, to the house of the God of Jacob; He will teach us His ways, and we shall walk in His paths." For out of Zion the law shall go forth, and the word of the Lord from Jerusalem.* (NKJV)

What a glorious prophetic promise that awaits us! May we be the generation that will witness the fulfillment of this promise. Every time a believer or church observes and celebrates the feast of Shavuot, they are declaring the prophetic fulfillment of the one new man. What a glorious thought.

Practical Guide to Celebrate Shavu'ot

As the celebration of Pentecost approaches, the individual house or church can be decorated with greenery, flowers, or sheaves of wheat to remind us of the harvest and first-fruits aspect. Then, as Erev Shavu'ot (the evening of Pentecost) approaches, family and friends gather around the festive table, the candles are lit, and the following blessing is recited:

Barukh atah Adonai Elohenu melakh ha-olam, asher kidshanu b'mitzvohtav l'hayot or l'goyeem V'natan-lanu Ye'shua m'sheekhaynu ha-or la-Olam.
(Blessed are you, O Lord our God, King of the universe, who has sanctified us by thy commandments and commanded us to be a light unto the nations and has given us Ye'shua, our Messiah, the light of the world.)

And then it is added:

Barukh atah Adonai Elohenu Melekh ha-olam, She-he-khiyanu v'kiya-manu vihigi-yanu lazman hazeh.
(Blessed are you, O Lord our God, King of the universe, who has given us life, sustained us, and brought us to this season.)

As an option, there is then a time of prayer focused on thanking God for the harvest of souls and asking God for the one new man to be established. Then the Kiddush blessings over the wine are spoken:

Baruch atah Adonai Elohenu melekh ha-olam, borayp'ree hagahfen.
(Blessed are you, O Lord our God, King of the universe, who creates the fruit of the vine.)

And then the challah bread is blessed:

Baruch atah Adonai Elohenu melekh ha-olam, ha-omotzee lekhem meen ha-aretz.
(Blessed are you, O Lord our God, King of the universe, who brings forth bread from the earth.)

The dinner is then served, which needs to include dairy products (like cheeses or cheese cake) to remind us of the milk of God's Word and the beauty of studying the Word of God.

Some churches may want to hold a special service on Erev Shavu'ot, or have an all-night study of the Word of God, specifically the first five books from Genesis to Deuteronomy, or simply read Scripture and discuss its principles. The other aspect is the outpouring of the Holy Spirit. This could be an extended time of worship and prayer for the baptism or infilling of the Holy Spirit and the cry for a revival to impact the church, city, and nation.

The Feast of Shavuot is very significant and can easily be celebrated by Gentile churches, bringing great blessing and fruitfulness to every participant.

The third pilgrim feast, as you will discover, is the most prophetic in nature and will inspire you to look for the return of the Messiah.

Rosh Hashanah

THE THIRD FEAST, THE FEAST OF TABERNACLES, WHICH REQUIRED all men to come to Yerushalayim, is actually preceded by Rosh Hashanah, the Jewish New Year. It is cited in Leviticus 23:24, where we read, *"In the seventh month, on the first day of the month, you shall have a sabbath-rest, a memorial of blowing of trumpets, a holy convocation"* (NKJV). On this day, one must not do any kind of ordinary work, and bring an offering made by fire to Adonai.

The Jewish Observance of Rosh Hashanah

The Jewish New Year is celebrated very differently than how the rest of the world celebrates the New Year. Rosh Hashanah, very simply, is translated as "the head of the year." The first day of the month of Tishri is believed by some Jewish scholars to be the anniversary of the creation of Adam in the Garden of Eden. At the beginning of every year, it is believed, according to the Talmud and repeated by oral tradition through the centuries, that all the inhabitants of the world pass before God like a flock of sheep; and it is decreed in the Heavenly court, who shall live and who shall die, who shall be impoverished and who shall be enriched, who shall fall and who shall rise.[3]

The principle difference with January 1 is that it is a time of repentance, reflection, and rest. It is a time of seriously presenting oneself before the Lord in humility, and devoting oneself to holiness and purity. Orthodox Jews are especially keen on observing Tevilah Mikveh, a special water immersion before entering the synagogue; this symbolizes cleansing their ways. The blasts of the shofar are called Yom Teruah (The Day of the Sounding/The Festival of Trumpets). Therefore, when the shofars sounded, it was a call to draw closer to God in repentance and humility, acknowledging God as King of the universe. The trumpet blast would often be used to announce and commemorate:

1. the coronation of the king.
2. a call to repentance, commemorating man's sin and his repentance.
3. the first of the ten Days of Awe leading to Yom Kippur, the Day of Atonement.
4. the binding of Isaac and the substitutionary ram that was sacrificed in Isaac's place.

---

[3] *The Talmud: A Selection* (New York, NY: Penguin Books, 2009).

I must mention the four different sounds of the shofar during Rosh Hashanah. They are as follows: *tekia* (blast), *shevarim* (broken notes or staccato), *teruah* (alarming blast), and the *tekiah gedolah* (the great blast). Interestingly, during a Rosh Hashanah service, the shofars are to be blown one hundred times. These four sounds of the shofar symbolize:

1. the hailing or coming of the King, who sits in judgment over His subjects.
2. the calling of troops to assemble for war.
3. a wake-up call, an alarm to call the people to an appointed time.

The significance is overwhelming when you consider the prophetic significance for the believer in Ye'shua. Consider this: Orthodox rabbis see a connection between the holy day of regathering and the coming of the Messiah. The historical emphasis of this holy day is repentance, but the prophetic theme looks to the future day when the full ingathering of God's people (the Jewish people) will occur because of the Messiah's advent.

The Chassidic community of ultra-Orthodox Jews to this day, in some circles, maintain that the State of Israel and its government are illegitimate because the Messiah has not yet come. They teach that when Messiah does come, He will gather the true Jews (according to them, only the Orthodox and observant Jews of the Torah) and then form a nation that will establish His rule from Jerusalem and thus begin the Messianic Age. For this reason, there are more Chassidic Jews living in New York City and the United States than in Israel at this time. The massive Chassidic community, known as the Lubavitchers, followed the teachings of the now-deceased Rabbi Menachem Mendel Schneerson, firmly believing that he was the Messiah and that he would lead them to Israel where he would be welcomed as the Messiah. There are even many who believe to this day that he will rise from the dead and unite all the faithful Jews around the world and establish a righteous nation that will embrace Halacha (Jewish Law) and implement its principles into the very fabric of the nation's conscience. Thus they shun the secular state of geopolitical Israel and refuse to abide by its guidelines and policies, and they will not send their young men and women to serve even in the IDF (the Israel Defense Forces).

The prayer focus during the time of Rosh Hashanah is to go like this: "God, give us a year of life, health, and prosperity in our family and community." Secondly, there is a time to speak the following blessing over each other: "L'Shana tova tikatei Veteichatim," which means "May you be inscribed and sealed for a good year." Lastly, many very devout Jews, when passing close to any body of water, will do Tashlich, which is a special prayer in which they declare to God, "And You shall cast their sins into the depth of the sea."

During the festive meal, families eat apples dipped in honey, symbolically portraying one's desire for a sweet year. As usual, they recite the Kiddush and the blessing pronounced over the challah bread.

The Correlation with the Second Coming of Ye'shua

"Let not your heart be troubled; you believe in God, believe also in Me. In My Father's house are many mansions; if it were not so, I would have told you. I go to prepare a place for you. And if I go and prepare a place for you, I will come again and receive you to Myself; that where I am, there you may be also. And where I go you know, and the way you know."

Thomas said to Him, "Lord, we do not know where You are going, and how can we know the way?"

Jesus said to him, "I am the way, the truth, and the life. No one comes to the Father except through Me." (John 14:1–6, NKJV)

The Apostle Paul declared in 1 Thessalonians 4:16–18:

For the Lord Himself will descend from heaven with a shout, with the voice of an archangel, and with the trumpet of God. And the dead in Christ will rise first. Then we who are alive and remain shall be caught up together with them in the clouds to meet the Lord in the air. And thus we shall always be with the Lord. Therefore comfort one another with these words. (NKJV)

Rosh Hashanah speaks to the believer in Ye'shua of the promise of the Second Coming of Jesus. Now, I do not want to enter into a discourse regarding the timing of His return, nor the eschatological positions that are very often the source of great contention among Bible scholars and denominations. I simply point out that the return of Ye'shua is foreshadowed by the Feast of Trumpets; the sounding of the shofar and the shout of the Archangel, as described by the Apostle Paul by revelation, is implied.

A second parallel scripture is found in 1 Corinthians 15:51–53.

> *Behold, I tell you a mystery: We shall not all sleep, but we shall all be changed—in a moment, in the twinkling of an eye, at the last trumpet. For the trumpet will sound, and the dead will be raised incorruptible, and we shall be changed. For this corruptible must put on incorruption, and this mortal must put on immortality.* (NKJV)

This scripture gives more clarity regarding the sounding of the trumpet (shofar) by declaring the timing of the Rapture. The last trumpet is very significant because it reveals and implies a comparison with the Roman army's bugle calls. The early church lived in a Roman world where imposing Roman legionnaires constantly made bugle calls. The Romans had three specific bugle calls. The first was a call to attention. The second was an order to form rank and get into position. The third, known as the last trumpet, was a signal to start marching. I believe we can see the parallel significance when the last trumpet sounds in the biblical context; it is heaven's order for us to leave this earth and meet the Lord in the air. Hallelujah!

The correlation of Rosh Hashanah and the second coming of Ye'shua is remarkable, so celebrating this feast in a local church is very significant. In a home or church, the shofars can be sounded, and a time of prayer and worship focused on repentance and humbling oneself before the Lord will have a positive impact upon the family and congregation for the coming year.

The Shemittah, the Sabbatical Year

> *Speak to the children of Israel, and say unto them: "The feasts of the Lord, which you shall proclaim to be holy convocations, these are My feasts [designated times]."* (Leviticus 23:1–2, NKJV)

The biblical calendar is observed and understood in seven-year cycles, and this cycle of time is applied to how we deal with the land and debt. The Shemittah very simply means "to release." Let's look at the Scriptures to understand this cycle and the mitzvahs, the commands of the Lord to Israel.

The Shemittah Kesafim, the Releasing of Debt

> *At the end of every seven years you shall grant a release of debts. And this is the form of the release: Every creditor who has lent anything to his neighbor shall release it; he*

> *shall not require it of his neighbor or his brother, because*
> *it is called the Lord's release [shemittah].* (Deuteronomy
> 15:1–2, NKJV)

Every Shemittah year was a time of great rejoicing for the one who was in debt, because God had set in place a system that would free individuals from the tyranny of debt. For six years, one would pay faithfully what he owed, but if he was not able to pay his entire debt because of hardship and trouble, God provided a way for the individual to be released from that burden. In a way, this was a display of God's mercy and grace. The picture is powerful: we owed a debt that we could not pay because of our sin; the penalty was eternal death, but God, who is rich in mercy, forgave our debt and delivered us from man's taskmaster, Satan, and the tyranny and oppression of sin.

The Shemittah Karko, the Year of Rest for the Land

> *Six years you shall sow your field, and six years you shall*
> *prune your vineyard, and gather its fruit; but in the*
> *seventh year there shall be a sabbath of solemn rest for the*
> *land, a sabbath to the Lord. You shall neither sow your*
> *field nor prune your vineyard. What grows of its own*
> *accord of your harvest you shall not reap, nor gather the*
> *grapes of your untended vine, for it is a year of rest for the*
> *land.* (Leviticus 25:3–5, NKJV)

In the seventh year, God commanded the people to not sow and plow the fields, so that the Land could replenish itself naturally by restoring all the nutrients that had been used up by the previous six years of sowing and harvesting. This was the natural consequence and its outcome, but God desired to remind Israel that they were to put their trust in God as their source. Even though ancient Israel was an agrarian culture that depended on the harvesting of crops to survive, God forced them to refocus and think about what is really important: their pursuit of a spiritual life that increases faith in God. The purpose was for them to focus less on material needs and recognize the priority of trusting God as their source.

Once again, the imagery is a powerful reminder that life is temporal and that the pursuit of temporal needs must never supersede our faith in God. Ye'shua Himself declared that we are to *"seek first the kingdom of God and His righteousness, and all these things shall be added to you"* (Matthew 6:33, NKJV). Notice that Jesus said *"all things"*—in other words, whatever you may need in life. Our human tendency is to worry and try to secure whatever is needed through our own effort and skill, but God calls us to trust and depend on Him, to proclaim that He is our source. This will definitely keep us humble and thankful, acknowledging that the world will continue to *"trust [in] chariots, and some in horses; but we will remember the name of the Lord our God"* (Psalm 20:7, NKJV). Horses and chariots metaphorically represent all the world's resources, which all humanity strives to acquire and place their security in. However, the man or woman who chooses to look to God as their source will truly find rest in their minds and freedom from the tyranny of worry. Friends, God will take care of you just as He told the people who questioned what would happen if they did not work their field in the seventh year. Notice these words in Leviticus 25:20–22:

> *And if you say, "What shall we eat in the seventh year, since we shall not sow nor gather in our produce?" Then I will command My blessing on you in the sixth year, and it will bring forth produce enough for three years. And you shall sow in the eighth year, and eat old produce until the ninth year; until its produce comes in, you shall eat of the old harvest.* (NKJV)

The Shemittah year is a unique year that opens a spiritual portal. The scriptural and spiritual implication is that there is a specific window (portal) of time when we can access the blessings and promises of God, which are available precisely because it is an appointed time, a set time for favor. You will do well to pay close attention to the Shemittah year.

Once again I remind you that there are seven-year cycles of time in God's biblical calendar, which is very significant. At the end of every Shemittah year, a new cycle of seven years begins. Now, if we are cognizant of the timing of the Shemittah, we can discern the sixth year and begin to sow accordingly, fully aware that we will enjoy three years of harvest as was revealed in Leviticus 25:20–22. You may not be a farmer in the physical sense, but that doesn't exclude you from experiencing the fulfilment of the promises of God.

Very simply, I believe that the decisions we make in the sixth year set the course for the next cycle of seven years. Some would say that I'm speculating and reading into Scripture, taking it out of context. Friends, I believe that the principles of Scripture transcend culture and time, but we are responsible to discern how it applies to our time and culture. Who we are today is the outcome of the decisions that served as defining moments in our past, setting in motion actions and events that have brought us to the present.

Therefore, consider the context of the seven-year cycle of the sabbath year of rest and release. When we walk in obedience to the Lord, acknowledging that He is our source and seeking first His kingdom in our lives, the decisions we make will affect us for the next seven years. I challenge you to ponder this truth and consider the application and implications in your life.

In closing this chapter, consider the principle of sowing and reaping, which is a universal irrevocable law in the Word of God. Galatians 6:7 declares, *"Do not be deceived, God is not mocked; for whatever a man sows, that he will also reap."*

Friends, if we sow financially in obedience to the Lord in the Shemittah year, the end result will be that we eat the old harvest for three years—until the ninth year, technically speaking. I encourage you to meditate on this powerful truth and ask the Ruach Ha Kodesh, the Holy Spirit, how it applies to you personally.

8

Yom Kippur

And the Lord spoke to Moses, saying: "Also the tenth day of this seventh month shall be the Day of Atonement. It shall be a holy convocation for you; you shall afflict your souls, and offer an offering made by fire to the Lord. And you shall do no work on that same day, for it is the Day of Atonement, to make atonement for you before the Lord your God... It shall be to you a sabbath of solemn rest, and you shall afflict your souls; on the ninth day of the month at evening, from evening to evening, you shall celebrate your sabbath." (Leviticus 23:26–28, 32, NKJV)

YOM KIPPUR, THE DAY OF ATONEMENT, IS CONSIDERED THE most holy day of the Bible calendar year. On this day, the High Priest would enter into the Holy of Holies and make atonement for the sin of the nation.

What began at Rosh Hashanah—namely, a time of repentance and self-evaluation—concluded ten days later with a day of atonement and regeneration. During the Temple Period in Hebrew history, this day was marked with an animal sacrifice and the presentation of blood sprinkled by the Cohen Hagadol (the High Priest) on the Kapparah, the mercy seat of the Ark of the Covenant within the Holy of Holies. Thus you can see the significance of the word Kippur, meaning to cover, to atone for. It was a day of fasting and prayer that brought to a close the ten days of Yomim Nora'im, the Days of Awe.

This was a very solemn time of reflection, repentance, and rest. As a side note, the Orthodox rabbis, no longer having a temple to offer the sacrifice, taught as a substitution the Tefilah (prayers), Teshuvah (repentance), and Tzedakah (charity)— in other words, the discipline of prayer with repentance and the giving of charity to provide for the poor and needy. These actions are the substitute, according to them, until the third temple is rebuilt and animal sacrifices are reinstated.

We know that Ye'shua fulfilled this and that there is no more need for vicarious animal sacrifices. The day can be observed at home with a festive meal on Erev Yom Kippur, the evening that commences the day. First there is a blessing of the wine with the Kiddush and the challah bread. The meal include sweets and a variety of deserts to commemorate the sweetness of forgiveness and restoration to God. The following twenty-four hours are observed with an absolute fast, meaning no liquids or solids for the duration. This holy day then ends with a meal in the home and a special service called a Neilah, which means "the closing of the gates." A final shofar blast signifies that that which has been established through repentance and humility is now sealed before the Lord.

Yom Kippur is truly a very solemn and significant time of reflection, repentance, and restoration for every believer in Ye'shua, whether Jew or Gentile.

9

Sukkot
(The Feast of Tabernacles)

AS YOU CAN SEE, THE MONTH OF TISHRI (SEPTEMBER–OCTOBER) is a very important time in the Jewish calendar. In the first nineteen days, there are three major holy days. The mood of somber repentance and reflection that was evident through Rosh Hashanah and Yom Kippur now culminates in eight days of remembrance and rejoicing.

Then the Lord spoke to Moses, saying, "Speak to the children of Israel, saying: 'The fifteenth day of this seventh month shall be the Feast of Tabernacles for seven days to the Lord. On the first day there shall be a holy convocation. You shall do no customary work on it. For seven days you shall offer an offering made by fire to the Lord. On the eighth day you shall have a holy convocation, and you shall offer an offering made by fire to the Lord. It is a sacred assembly, and you shall do no customary work on it.'" (Leviticus 23:33–36, NKJV)

I believe it is very important that we highlight the duration of this feast. In the Scriptures, names, numbers, and dates carry great significance, generally speaking. Adonai Elohim is a God of order and timing. He does nothing out of His timetable. This is very often why there arises conflict when putting one's trust in God! Very simply, the problem is our inability to discern God's timing and ordained process! As humans, we live in the world of the finite, the limited, the confined, and we are within the scope of time and space.

Consider God the Creator. He is infinite, unlimited, and definitely not confined by time and space. He is not subject or bound to the rules of the physical universe. The Scriptures go to great lengths to establish God's greatness in a language we can understand. However, at best they still fall short of accurately describing His greatness. King David declared in Psalms 8:3–4,

When I consider Your heavens, the work of Your fingers, the moon and the stars, which You have ordained, what is man that You are mindful of him, and the son of man that You visit him? (NKJV)

David was utterly amazed at the greatness of God, as well as His concern and love for mere human beings. It was as if David was caught in a time and thought bubble, fully cognizant of God's vastness as the Creator.

In the book of Job, Elohim confronts Job and speaks to him out of the storm, challenging Job to consider the unsearchable, unfathomable greatness of the Creator. He begins by asking Job questions:

> *Where were you when I laid the foundations of the earth? Tell Me, if you have understanding. Who determined its measurements? Surely you know! Or who stretched the line upon it? To what were its foundations fastened? Or who laid its cornerstone, when the morning stars sang together, and all the sons of God shouted for joy?* (Job 38:4–7, NKJV)

Obviously, Job was at a loss for words, because he realized that you cannot figure God out through human reasoning and intellect. The sooner we embrace this truth, the quicker we will be settled in our faith in God. Nonetheless, God said to Moses that creation happened in seven days, which speaks to the fullness of one week. The number seven has been understood as the number of God. The Prophet Isaiah describes Adonai Elohim in His fullness:

> *The Spirit of the Lord shall rest upon Him, the Spirit of wisdom and understanding, the Spirit of counsel and might, the Spirit of knowledge and of the fear of the Lord. His delight is in the fear of the Lord, and He shall not judge by the sight of His eyes, nor decide by the hearing of His ears; but with righteousness He shall judge the poor, and decide with equity for the meek of the earth; He shall strike the earth with the rod of His*

mouth, and with the breath of His lips He shall slay the wicked. (Isaiah 11:2–4, NKJV)

Revelation 5:1–6 says,

And I saw in the right hand of Him who sat on the throne a scroll written inside and on the back, sealed with seven seals. Then I saw a strong angel proclaiming with a loud voice, "Who is worthy to open the scroll and to loose its seals?"…

But one of the elders said to me, "Do not weep. Behold, the Lion of the tribe of Judah, the Root of David, has prevailed to open the scroll and to loose its seven seals."

And I looked, and behold, in the midst of the throne and of the four living creatures, and in the midst of the elders, stood a Lamb as though it had been slain, having seven horns and seven eyes, which are the seven Spirits of God sent out into all the earth. (Revelation 5:1–2, 5–6, NKJV)

Here very clearly is the confirmation of what Isaiah said eight hundred years before the birth of Ye'shua. John, on the Isle of Patmos, had a heavenly experience where the number seven again came to the forefront; there were seven seals, seven horns, seven eyes, and the sevenfold Spirit of God! It is clear to me that this final feast of Sukkot—seven days of celebration and remembrance—speaks of the fullness of God's timetable.

The prophet Zechariah prophesied eschatologically and apocalyptically of the end and culmination of God's plan. He speaks of the final conflagration and siege of the city of Yerushalayim, when the nations will gather as one to destroy the Jewish state and God Himself will intervene to destroy the invading armies:

And it shall come to pass that everyone who is left of all the nations which came against Jerusalem shall go up from year to year to worship the King, the Lord of hosts, and to keep the Feast of Tabernacles. And it shall be that whichever of the families of the earth do not come up to Jerusalem to worship the King, the Lord of hosts, on them there will be no rain. If the family of Egypt will not come up and enter in, they shall have no rain; they shall receive the plague with which the Lord strikes the nations who do not come up to keep the Feast of Tabernacles. (Zechariah 14:16–18, NKJV)

Wow! Consider that this festival is the only one that will be observed when the Messiah comes and establishes His reign from Yerushalayim. If you look back to the other two feasts of the Regalim—or the Pilgrim Feasts, both Pesach (Passover) and Shavu'ot (Pentecost)—you will have cause to remember and repent! However, Sukkot calls us to remember and look forward to the fullness of God's Kingdom on earth. In other words, the festival of Sukkot points to the return of the Messiah. Therefore, the themes of harvest and celebration are highlighted as we eat and dwell under the temporary *sukkah* (booths), which remind us that this world is our temporary dwelling. As believers, this festival is the one of promise; we can safely declare that Ye'shua may actually come in the Rapture during the physical feast of Sukkot. The parallels are unmistakable; His first coming was during this time and His second coming will also occur during this time. As a reminder, the biblical birth of Jesus did not happen on December 25; more likely it was in September/October, during the festival of Sukkot.

Sukkot Observance and Meaning

This festival is referred to with different names that speak of the various aspects of this time, the Zeman Simhatenu, the Season of our Joy (also known as the Feast of Ingathering), the Feast of Booths (Tabernacles), and the Nissuch Ha-Mayim (which means "the pouring of water"). The greatest day is the eighth, called the Hosheanah Rabbah, the Great Hosanna!

Now let's consider the finer details.

Sukkah (Booths)

Leviticus 23:42–43 declares,

> *You shall dwell in booths for seven days. All who are native Israelites shall dwell in booths, that your generations may know that I made the children of Israel dwell in*

*booths when I brought them out of the land of Egypt:
I am the Lord your God.* (NKJV)

The temporary, vulnerable, and fragile leaves and shelters which were made of freshly cut palm branches or willow branches had the smell of myrtle, reminding them of the faithfulness of God during the forty years of wandering in the desert. In more modern cities and homes made out of brick and mortar, it was easy to forget the time of wandering and instability in the desert.

The word Sukkah originally meant "woven," because these branches were temporarily sewn together to provide shade for livestock. They provided a resting place for warriors and a temporary shade from the hot sun for guards during the harvest.

This feast coincided with Israel's final harvest of the year. Consider for a moment the impact of Israel's economy during the biblical era. It was an agricultural economy; there was no industry, no office buildings or extensive foreign trade. Life revolved around the seasons and the raising of crops. The rain decreed their provisions from year to year. Twenty-first-century North American society doesn't understand the impact of a year with little or no rain; we have an abundance of international trade and relief organizations that would step in and alleviate the burden of lack. However, in ancient Israel, if the harvest was plentiful, it brought great joy and a renewed sense of relief and thankfulness to God for His provision. This was a great cause to rejoice and feast before the Lord. The

Hebrew word for feast (*hag*) means "to dance or to be joyous," and it applies exclusively to the three pilgrim feasts: Pesach (Passover), Shavu'ot (Pentecost), and Sukkot (Tabernacles).

Spiritual and Physical Application

Through the observance of the feast, the Lord was teaching the people to not forget His goodness and faithfulness during the years of transition in the desert. He was reminding them how He had provided, protected, and preserved them in a harsh and hostile environment during a difficult season of life. It is very easy to forget where we came from when we are doing well, when we are settled, comfortable, prospering, and living in leisure.

Immigrants to North America can relate a little bit, having left their countries and nations of birth to find fortune and a better life for their families and children. Every immigrant remembers the challenges and sacrifices of their earlier days, the cultural difficulties and expectations, a different mindset and language, the demands of a society that's not so forgiving, and at times they were subject to racial and cultural discrimination. They sometimes feel humiliation and ridicule because they don't express themselves well and can't read simple instructions to fill out forms just to receive help. Every immigrant remembers the early seasons of their lives in the immigration process, and many of them *want* to forget. But they now enjoy the blessing of homes, properties, businesses, cottages, boats, cars, and the accomplishments of their children, who have the opportunity to excel in careers that they themselves could only dream of once upon a time. How far their families have come!

Zeman Simhatenu: The Season of Joy

This is the season of joy, Zeman Simhatenu, a time to not forget our history and dependence on God. Sukkot was an intentional reminder to Israel to reflect on the goodness of God. The human inclination is to forget the difficult past and become proud and haughty, thinking to ourselves, *Look at what I have achieved and accomplished with no one's help. I'm a self-made man!* This thinking reveals a violation of the foundational principle of our need to recognize God's sovereignty in our lives, and at its root is the seed of pride, which God resists and abhors.

God spoke to Israel through Moses in Deuteronomy 6:10–12, saying,

> *So it shall be, when the Lord your God brings you into the land of which He swore to your fathers, to Abraham, Isaac, and Jacob, to give you large and beautiful cities which you did not build, houses full of all good things, which you did not fill, hewn-out wells which you did not dig, vineyards and olive trees which you did not plant—when you have eaten and are full—then beware, lest you forget the Lord who brought you out of the land of Egypt, from the house of bondage.* (NKJV)

Moses continues to proclaim God's warning to Israel in Deuteronomy 8:11–18, saying,

Beware that you do not forget the Lord your God by not keeping His commandments, His judgments, and His statutes which I command you today, lest—when you have eaten and are full, and have built beautiful houses and dwell in them; and when your herds and your flocks multiply, and your silver and your gold are multiplied, and all that you have is multiplied; when your heart is lifted up, and you forget the Lord your God who brought you out of the land of Egypt, from the house of bondage; who led you through that great and terrible wilderness, in which were fiery serpents and scorpions and thirsty land where there was no water; who brought water for you out of the flinty rock; who fed you in the wilderness with manna, which your fathers did not know, that He might humble you and that He might test you, to do you good in the end—then you say in your heart, "My power and the might of my hand have gained me this wealth."

And you shall remember the Lord your God, for it is He who gives you power to get wealth, that He may establish His covenant which He swore to your fathers, as it is this day. (NKJV)

The feast's warning is clear: Do not forget!

Water Libation Ceremony (Nissuch Ha-Mayim)

Once again, Sukkot was an eight-day festival with significant observances that commemorated the goodness and faithfulness of God. The pouring of the water ceremony was also a joyous occasion that prophetically spoke of the outpouring of the Holy Spirit.

The ceremony began with a Levitical priest, appointed specifically for that day, with a golden pitcher descending from the temple, making his way to the pool of Siloam to draw water. As he made his way down, he was accompanied by flutists and worshippers. Upon filling his pitcher, he would begin his ascent towards the temple mount through the Water Gate, welcomed by the blowing of the shofars. When he entered the temple, he proceeded to the southwest corner of the altar, where two bowls were placed. One bowl, on the eastern side, was filled with wine for the drink offering. The second bowl, on the western side, was for the water. As the priest poured the water, the worshippers, accompanied by flutes, declared, *"Save now, I pray, O Lord; O Lord, I pray, send now prosperity"* (Psalm 118:25, NKJV). As these words were recited, the people waved their palm branches towards the altar until the water was completely poured out.

Now, consider what took place when Jesus entered Jerusalem on a white donkey. On the day of His triumphal entry, the Bible says that the crowds welcomed Him waving palm branches, shouting, *"Hosanna to the Son of David! 'Blessed is He who comes in the name of the Lord!' Hosanna in the highest!"* (Matthew 21:9, NKJV) The crowds shouted, "Lord, save us!" Jesus fulfilled to a tee even this part of the festival, showing the significance of the prayer for deliverance.

The Crying Out for the Spirit

The drawing of the water ceremony also presented an aspect that is very prophetic in nature, and that is the cry of the people for the Spirit of God to be poured out upon the Land. Joel 2:23–25 says,

> *Be glad then, you children of Zion, and rejoice in the Lord your God; for He has given you the former rain faithfully, and He will cause the rain to come down for you—the former rain, and the latter rain in the first month. The threshing floors shall be full of wheat, and the vats shall overflow with new wine and oil. So I will restore to you the years that the swarming locust has eaten, the crawling locust, the consuming locust, and the chewing locust, my great army which I sent among you.* (NKJV)

This was the prophetic promise of the Spirit coming like rain upon the land. The result was a harvest of grain, wine, and oil—and then a restoration of the years that the locusts had consumed. I think it would be appropriate to bring application and significance to the three symbols of grain, wine, and oil in the context of the Holy Spirit.

The grain. The grain represents the harvest of souls, people coming into the Kingdom of God. Jesus told the parable of a farmer who sowed wheat into his field, and at night an enemy came and sowed tares (weeds). In the parable, the farmer said,

Let both grow together until the harvest, and at the time of harvest I will say to the reapers, "First gather together the tares and bind them in bundles to burn them, but gather the wheat into my barn." (Matthew 13:30, NKJV)

Jesus proceeded to say that the harvEsthers were angels, the wheat were the righteous, and the tares represented the wicked (see Matthew 13:24–30; 36–43). So it is clear that grain was used as a metaphor for people.

The wine. Wine in Scripture very often represents the joy of the Holy Spirit, the renewing and refreshing of the Spirit of God. New wine in Scripture represents the outpouring of the Holy Spirit. Right through the Tanach (Old Testament), the metaphor of new wine is used to describe the season of joy. Acts 2 records what transpired when the Holy Spirit was poured out; those who had gathered to witness and hear the crowd speaking in tongues mocked them, saying, *"They are full of new wine"* (Acts 2:13, NKJV). The Apostle Peter, a natural spokesman, raised his voice to dispel this criticism:

For these are not drunk, as you suppose, since it is only the third hour of the day. But this is what was spoken by the

prophet Joel: "And it shall come to pass in the last days, says God, that I will pour out of My Spirit on all flesh; your sons and your daughters shall prophesy, your young men shall see visions, your old men shall dream dreams. And on My menservants and on My maidservants I will pour out My Spirit in those days; and they shall prophesy." (Acts 2:15–18, NKJV)

Notice the comparison of the physical, visual, and spiritual reality! The Apostle Peter identifies the outpouring of the Holy Spirit, confirming the fulfillment of Joel 3:1–2—or, in the NKJV, Joel 2:28–29. All of this is in the context of joy and the symbolism of new wine.

The oil. The metaphor of oil was very clearly a reference to the Holy Spirit's effect of healing and restoration. Oil, I must add, was also a symbol of being set apart for holiness, or the anointing of a prophet, priest, or king. I believe the connection specifically speaks of the anointing of the Holy Spirit to restore life, healing, and wholeness again to God's people. The prophet Isaiah clearly spoke about the symbolism of drawing out the water and the declaration of the Lord's faithfulness:

And in that day you will say: "O Lord, I will praise You; though You were angry with me, Your anger is turned away, and You comfort me. Behold, God is my salvation, I will trust and not be afraid; 'For Yah, the Lord, is my strength and song; He also has become my salvation.'"

Therefore with joy you will draw water from the wells of salvation.

And in that day you will say: "Praise the Lord, call upon His name; declare His deeds among the peoples, make mention that His name is exalted. Sing to the Lord, for He has done excellent things; this is known in all the earth. Cry out and shout, O inhabitant of Zion, for great is the Holy One of Israel in your midst!" (Isaiah 12:1–6, NKJV)

Through the water-drawing ceremony, the worshippers would recite these words: "May God send His Spirit upon us now." The Talmud, the Jewish commentary of the Scriptures, adds, "Why is the name of this ceremony called the drawing out of water? Because of the pouring out of the Holy Spirit according to Isaiah 12:3."

The final part of this weeklong feast was called the day of Hosheanah Rabbah, the Great Hosanna. This was a cry from the very heart and soul of God's people for salvation. The word Hosheanah literally means, "Lord, save us now." If it had been a very bad year for the crops, there had been a lack of rain, or if the people were living under a foreign occupation, the cry of the people would be, "Save us now!" On this final day, the priest leading the ceremony would encircle the altar of sacrifice seven times and the people would cry out Hosheanah seven times.

The Prophetic Fulfilment with Ye'shua

The Scriptures record specifically that Jesus attended the feast of Sukkot. The Apostle John records,

> *On the last day, that great day of the feast, Jesus stood and cried out, saying, "If anyone thirsts, let him come to Me and drink. He who believes in Me, as the Scripture has said, out of his heart will flow rivers of living water." But this He spoke concerning the Spirit, whom those believing in Him would receive; for the Holy Spirit was not yet given, because Jesus was not yet glorified.* (John 7:37–39, NKJV)

Here we see the prophetic fulfillment as Jesus declares openly that He is Israel's salvation. The symbolism of drinking the water and the outpouring of the Spirit powerfully points to salvation in Ye'shua, the Messiah. Life in its fullness can only be accessed through coming to Ye'shua.

Now consider the prophetic words of Isaiah 55, for it is a foreshadowing of the Messiah and His connection with the Feast of Sukkot:

> *"Ho! Everyone who thirsts, come to the waters; and you who have no money, come, buy and eat. Yes, come, buy wine and milk without money and without price. Why do you spend money for what is not bread, and your wages for what does not satisfy? Listen carefully to Me, and eat what is good, and let your soul delight itself in abundance. Incline your*

ear, and come to Me. Hear, and your soul shall live; and I will make an everlasting covenant with you—the sure mercies of David. (Isaiah 55:1–3, NKJV)

Notice that this is the exact same invitation Jesus gave on that great day when He said, "Come if you are thirsty."

The next few verses confirm the theme of salvation. Isaiah declares,

Seek the Lord while He may be found, call upon Him while He is near. Let the wicked forsake his way, and the unrighteous man his thoughts; let him return to the Lord, and He will have mercy on him; and to our God, for He will abundantly pardon. (Isaiah 55:6–7, NKJV)

The promise of forgiveness and salvation is assured and confirmed if Israel or any one individual comes to the Messiah in repentance and humility. The cry of God's heart is for His people to return to Him with a genuine desire to walk in His ways and display His lordship and sovereignty in their lives. The Old and New Covenants correlate and confirm the same themes and truths.

A Theological Inconsistency

Let me address this very principle. To properly exegete and understand God's revelation of Himself and His plan, one requires both the Old and New Testaments.

You cannot separate the two, assuming that the New Testament has replaced the Old and that therefore the Old Testament Scriptures are now irrelevant and obsolete. Their theological perspective is similar to a contractor building a house without a foundation in place. Doing so would be ridiculous, yet over and over throughout church history we have witnessed erroneous views of Israel and the Jewish people, views which contribute to antisemitic hostility. The root cause originates with a devaluation of the entirety of Scripture.

Therefore, it is safe to say that the enemy (Satan) has succeeded through history, and even in some Christian denominations today, in sowing doubt and questioning the authentic authority of the Bible. The end result has been the creation of a great divide between Israel and the Christian church. Thank God that many in the circles of the church are beginning to identify the seeds of antisemitism through wrong theology and are committing themselves to restoring a right understanding of the role and place of Israel and the Jewish people in God's plan.

The Prophetic Fulfilment with Ye'shua Continued

The next few verses speak about the water of the Spirit being translated through the Word of God and the subsequent result of coming to the Messiah and drinking His water. Isaiah 55:8–13 says,

"For My thoughts are not your thoughts, nor are your ways My ways," says the Lord. "For as the heavens are higher than the earth, so are My ways higher than your ways, and My thoughts than your thoughts.

"For as the rain comes down, and the snow from heaven, and do not return there, but water the earth, and make it bring forth and bud, that it may give seed to the sower and bread to the eater, so shall My word be that goes forth from My mouth; it shall not return to Me void, but it shall accomplish what I please, and it shall prosper in the thing for which I sent it.

"For you shall go out with joy, and be led out with peace; the mountains and the hills shall break forth into singing before you, and all the trees of the field shall clap their hands. Instead of the thorn shall come up the cypress tree, and instead of the brier shall come up the myrtle tree; and it shall be to the Lord for a name, for an everlasting sign that shall not be cut off."
(NKJV)

Notice the consequent result of the abundance of rain: lush trees and vegetation will grow, replacing thorns and briars that grow in arid places. Also notice the restoration of joy, metaphorically described through the creation responding to the rain. The spiritual parallel is so apparent; when Israel, or any individual, receives the rain of God's Spirit in their lives by coming to Ye'shua the Messiah, their lives, which were spiritually dry and dead, will come to life. Add to this a picture of fruitfulness and blessing, causing the Word of God, accompanied by the rain of the Spirit, to *"bring forth and bud, that it may give seed to the sower and the bread to the eater"* (Isaiah 55:10, NKJV), causing the individual to experience great joy because of embracing God's Word.

Once again consider the principle of sowing and reaping—from heaven's perspective this time. Rain is sown onto the earth, providing seed for the sower, which then grows up into a harvest of grain, which is then transformed into bread that satisfies our bodies' need for food. Just as the rain of the Holy Spirit is poured out upon a life, family, and church, the end result is a harvest of souls, blessing, and righteousness. What a powerful truth!

The Foreshadowing of the One New Man in Isaiah

Another Scripture often bypassed and poorly understood is Isaiah 44:1–5, which says,

> *Yet hear now, O Jacob My servant, and Israel whom I have chosen. Thus says the Lord who made you and formed you from the womb, who will help you: "Fear not, O Jacob My servant; and you, Jeshurun, whom I have chosen. For I will pour water on him who is thirsty, and floods on the dry ground; I will pour My Spirit on your descendants, and My blessing on your offspring; they will spring up among the grass like willows by the watercourses." One will say, "I am the Lord's"; another will call himself by the name of*

*Jacob; another will write with his hand, "The Lord's," and
name himself by the name of Israel.* (NKJV)

The prophet Isaiah identifies and addresses Israel as
"Jacob My servant," the one whom the Lord has chosen. The
promise is that God will pour out His Spirit like water on the
thirsty land, the streams, and the dry ground, representing
the descendants and offspring of Jacob. Notice the prophetic
fulfillment, that they will spring up like grass and willows
on the riverbanks. Have you ever stopped to gaze upon the
multiplied blades of grass and willows? They number in the
millions. The picture given here is that the descendants of
Jacob will be too numerous to count.

Today, if you were to seek to count the physical
descendants of Jacob, it would be in the millions. The
estimate for those who are observant Jews or fully immersed
in Judaism is more than thirteen million. Add to this number
those who are intermarried or from a Jewish lineage, as well
as the multiplied millions of dispersed Jews through history
who became *Conversos*, a Spanish word to describe those who
left their Jewish identity to preserve their lives and families.
When you stop to consider the physical descendants of Jacob
alone, the number cannot fully be counted.

For a moment, consider with me the spiritual descendants
of Abraham, the Gentiles that through Jesus, the seed of
Abraham, have now been grafted in! The numbers are
staggering to consider. The prophet Isaiah saw this happening,
by declaring,

> *One will say, "I am the Lord's"; another will call himself by*
> *the name of Jacob; another will write with his hand,*
> *"The Lord's," and name himself by the name of Israel.*
> (Isaiah 44:5, NKJV)

I believe that this reference speaks of the physical descendants of Jacob. The other refers to the Gentiles who belong to the Lord and who will *"adopt the surname Isra'el"* (Isaiah 44:5, CJB). Here we clearly see the one new man prophesied by Isaiah in an embryonic form, eight hundred years before the coming of Jesus and the inauguration of the church recorded in Acts 2:2.

The Four Symbols of Sukkot

During the feast, especially on the last day, observant Jews held in their hands four things as they came to the synagogue or Western Wall in Jerusalem. First of all, they would have a *lulav*, comprised of a cluster of willow, myrtle, and palm branches used for the purpose of waving in great rejoicing during the festival, or specifically during the day of the priestly blessing. The second object is the *etrog*, an Aramaic word which means "that which shines"; it is a citrus fruit, the citron, a fragrant golden oblong fruit larger than a lemon.

These four emblems speak to us about the human body, and what the Lord requires of us in our service to Him.

1. Etrog represents the heart, the place of understanding and wisdom, the very place where our core decisions are made.
2. Lulav represents the backbone of a person, and the cluster tied together speaks of their uprightness of character, integrity, and righteousness.
3. Myrtle corresponds to the eyes; it speaks of vision and enlightenment and the need for clarity in life.
4. Willow represents the lips, and the service of our lips in prayer and worship to God.

These four emblems represent a person's life and devotion to God. Even though these observances are traditional and nonbiblical, they still serve a vital purpose. First of all, they serve as a reminder that our rejoicing and thanksgiving requires our whole being. For example, God requires worship from your body, soul, and spirit. Secondly, it is a good visual to teach the younger generation of the requirements of a good life, a life that is pleasing to HaShem! And that, my friends, is a very good thing.

Sukkot Eschatologically

When we speak of eschatology, we are referring to the study of the end times. I believe that it would be good for me to qualify what I am about to address by sharing with you a simple premise: the theology of eschatology cannot be presented in a dogmatic way. I believe that the Scriptures give us highlights of what will happen, but we cannot say that events will take place exactly this way or that way. Nor can we clearly, unequivocally foresee the chronological sequence of events, or their frequency. We may simply identify what the Scriptures reveal and qualify our interpretation of these events by stating our opinions without presenting them as doctrine.

Consider what the Scriptures reveal about Sukkot and the celebration of this feast in Jerusalem during the end of days. The prophet Zechariah describes a time prior to the return of the Messiah when the nations will gather against Jerusalem and Israel to plunder and destroy the Jewish people. At that time, the Lord Himself will come as the Captain of the hosts of heaven and place His feet on the Mount of Olives and establish His kingdom from Jerusalem, reigning over all the earth. Once judgment and justice have been served, the nations of the world will come to celebrate and observe the feast of Sukkot in Jerusalem. Notice what Zechariah saw:

And it shall come to pass that everyone who is left of all the nations which came against Jerusalem shall go up from year to year to worship the King, the Lord of hosts, and to keep the Feast of Tabernacles. And it shall be that whichever of the families of the earth do not come up to Jerusalem to worship the King, the Lord of hosts, on them there will be no rain. If the family of Egypt will not come up and enter in, they shall have no rain; they shall receive the plague with which the Lord strikes the nations who do not come up to keep the Feast of Tabernacles. This shall be the punishment of Egypt and the punishment of all the nations that do not come up to keep the Feast of Tabernacles. (Zechariah 14:16–19, NKJV)

From this prophetic scripture, the only biblical feast that will be celebrated when Ye'shua returns during His Millennial Reign will be Sukkot. Amazingly, the nations will come and gather before the King and worship the Messiah. Notice the parallels of Sukkot, past and present, with the future, including the theme of the ingathering of the harvest, the first-fruits, and the inauguration of the church. Now consider the future celebration; nations will gather and worship the Lord, acknowledging the mercy and goodness of God through His grace. What a glorious time that will be, rejoicing in the presence of the King!

The future is glorious, and by celebrating Sukkot you are prophetically declaring that the day of fulfillment is coming, that the Messiah is going to return and establish His Kingdom.

Conclusion: A Final Look at Leviticus 23:39–43

Adonai declares,

Also on the fifteenth day of the seventh month, when you have gathered in the fruit of the land, you shall keep the feast of the Lord for seven days; on the first day there shall be a sabbath-rest, and on the eighth day a sabbath-rest. And you shall take for yourselves on the first day the fruit of beautiful trees, branches of palm trees, the boughs of leafy trees, and willows of the brook; and you shall rejoice before the Lord your God for seven days. You shall keep it as a feast to the Lord for seven days in the year. It shall be a statute forever in your generations. You shall celebrate it in the seventh month. You shall dwell in booths for seven days. All who are native Israelites shall dwell in booths, that your generations may know that I made the children of Israel dwell in booths when I brought them out of the land of Egypt: I am the Lord your God. (Leviticus 23:39–43, NKJV)

Once again, the theme of Sukkot is to remind the people of the goodness of God and His grace, provision, and protection through the year. It is a reminder that our journeys are temporal and fragile. The shelters made of palm branches and willows provided for Israel an object lesson, that we cannot place our trust in temporary, fragile, material things. Our source of provision, protection, and preservation is the Lord Himself. Everything in life can be removed or taken away, because nothing is permanent and constant. Only when we live with this truth fully embraced will our focus be the Lord Himself and His truth.

Sukkot is truly a very important feast that will be celebrated and observed even when Ye'shua comes and reigns from Yerushalayim as King over the earth.

Purim, the Story of Deliverance

THE FEAST OF PURIM IS NOT CONSIDERED ONE OF THE MAJOR feasts to be observed, but it nonetheless carries great significance. It recalls a time in history, approximately around 450 B.C. in the ancient empire of Persia (Iran), when the very survival of the Jewish people hung in the balance. Historically, the Babylonians had deported many Jews, who had settled everywhere in the Middle East, and by the time the Persian Empire had replaced the Babylonian the Jews were fully assimilated and prosperous in their countries of residence.

Very simply, the story recorded in the book of Esther speaks of the great deliverance and protection of God from a cruel and wicked descendant of the Amalekites who had come to power and influence. His name was Haman.

Now, I believe it is important to share some insights to help us fully appreciate the protection of God and why evil must be dealt with immediately or else it will return later to destroy us. To understand this principle, we need to go back

to the time of Israel's return to the land after their deliverance
from Egyptian slavery.

In Exodus 17, while the nation was camped at Refidim
and the people began to murmur and complain because of
thirst, God provided water, through a rock, but in the context
of quarrelling and unbelief. After this episode of testing, the
Amalakites attacked an indefensible people. Consider what
Scripture says about this battle:

> *Now Amalek came and fought with Israel in
> Rephidim. And Moses said to Joshua, "Choose us some
> men and go out, fight with Amalek. Tomorrow I will
> stand on the top of the hill with the rod of God in my
> hand." So Joshua did as Moses said to him, and fought
> with Amalek. And Moses, Aaron, and Hur went up to
> the top of the hill. And so it was, when Moses held up his
> hand, that Israel prevailed; and when he let down his
> hand, Amalek prevailed. But Moses' hands became heavy;
> so they took a stone and put it under him, and he sat on
> it. And Aaron and Hur supported his hands, one on one
> side, and the other on the other side; and his hands were
> steady until the going down of the sun. So Joshua defeated
> Amalek and his people with the edge of the sword.*
>
> *Then the Lord said to Moses, "Write this for a
> memorial in the book and recount it in the hearing of
> Joshua, that I will utterly blot out the remembrance of
> Amalek from under heaven." And Moses built an altar
> and called its name, The-Lord-Is-My-Banner; for he said,*

"Because the Lord has sworn: the Lord will have war with Amalek from generation to generation." (Exodus 17:8–16, NKJV)

This was the first battle that the descendants of Jacob physically fought after four hundred years of Egyptian slavery. It immediately followed a time of contention and disunity at the waters of M'rivah (meaning "to quarrel") at a place called Massah (meaning "to test"). It was an unbearable time for this fledging nation, wandering with women and children and their herds and flocks. They had no natural protection of walled cities or fortresses, and the Amalekites decided to take advantage of this vulnerability and wipe them out right in the desert.

What must be considered is that Amalek's motivation to destroy Israel at its weakest moment was one of hatred, inspired by evil. Why do I say that? Very simply, when God promised the land of Canaan to Israel and commanded them to wipe out the inhabitants west of the Jordan River, the Amalekites were not on the list to be dispossessed and destroyed. So it is clear that this unprovoked attack was not motivated by a need to defend their nation, nor was it motivated by fear, because they had nothing to fear from the Israelites. Amalek, simply put, became the enemy, inspired by a hatred for the Jews and fueled by an antisemitic spirit. This unprovoked attack revealed the wickedness of these people, which gave access to the demonic strategy to wipe out God's chosen people. For this reason, God says,

I will utterly blot out the remembrance of Amalek from under heaven… Because the Lord has sworn: the Lord will have war with Amalek from generation to generation. (Exodus 17:14, 16, NKJV)

Following through a number of generations, once again Israel found itself facing the Amalekites, this time by a direct order from the Lord, given to King Saul, to wipe out this people once and for all. In 1 Samuel 15:2–3, Shmu'el the seer speaks to King Saul:

Thus says the Lord of hosts: "I will punish Amalek for what he did to Israel, how he ambushed him on the way when he came up from Egypt. Now go and attack Amalek, and utterly destroy all that they have, and do not spare them. But kill both man and woman, infant and nursing child, ox and sheep, camel and donkey." (NKJV)

It would seem very harsh and cruel to hear this command from the Lord if our only grid of understanding the nature of God was love. We forget too often that our God is also a God of justice. Added to that truth is that He is a God who keeps covenant.

The Lord called Isra'el the apple of His eye, and whoever would seek to do harm to the apple of His eye would find themselves coming up against God Himself. We forget that God's judgment is an expression of His mercy. Consider for a moment: if God did not judge wickedness and sin, how could He continue to be the moral judge of the universe? This would be inconsistent with His nature. Critics will continue to accuse the God of the Bible as being cruel, despotic, and outright vengeful. They seek every opportunity to discredit the authenticity of the Scriptures. But a child of God sees the goodness of God in protecting His people.

Now, returning to Amalek, the end result was that King Saul partially obeyed God:

> *But Saul and the people spared Agag and the best of the sheep, the oxen, the fatlings, the lambs, and all that was good, and were unwilling to utterly destroy them. But everything despised and worthless, that they utterly destroyed.* (1 Samuel 15:9, NKJV)

The Bible records that God was very displeased with Sha'ul's disobedience, and chose to strip the kingship from him to give to a better man (see 1 Samuel 15:10–23). Seeking to unpack this episode, consider the severity of God's judgment against Saul; it may seem that it was unfair, especially when you consider the gravity of King David's sin of adultery with Bathsheba and the conspiracy to murder her husband Uriah. David's punishment was the death of the child, but he did not lose his kingdom! So what was the difference? Very simply, King Saul's act of mercy put at risk the survival of the Jewish people, whereas David's sin was a personal weakness that affected Bathsheba and the child alone.

King Saul, in choosing to spare King Agag, also entitled his entire family to be spared. After the arrival of the prophet Samuel, Agag was called in and Samuel himself hacked him to pieces before the Lord. Agag's family—his wife and all his children—was still spared. Therefore, the Amalekite nation, the sworn enemies of Israel, survived because of King Saul's disobedience.

Fast-forward into the future and observe the connection of Amalek to the feast of Purim.

The Jewish people enter the Diaspora after the exile and the story focuses on a young beautiful Jewess named Hadassah, though she was given a Persian name to hide her Jewish identity. Esther was the niece of Mordecai, a very influential Jew in the court of the king. Interestingly, Mordecai could very possibly be the first "court Jew," a term used during the Middle Ages in Europe, when kings and barons ruled their fiefdoms, hiring court Jews as counsellors and advisors.

Esther was chosen to be the queen because of God's favor, so she found herself uniquely positioned at this time to be the vessel of deliverance for the Jewish people from the greatest threat of annihilation since their days in Egypt. The Bible says in Esther 3:1 that a man was quickly rising to power and influence in the Kingdom called Haman, the son of Hamdata the Agagite. This man was the direct descendant of Agag the Amalekite. As you read the scroll of Esther, you will discover that this Agagite never forgot what Israel did to the Amalekites. Vengeance and unbridled hatred burned in his bloodline. Haman found an excuse to begin plotting to destroy the Jewish people because Mordecai refused to bow and pay him homage. In Esther 3:6, we read,

> *But he disdained to lay hands on Mordecai alone, for they had told him of the people of Mordecai. Instead, Haman sought to destroy all the Jews who were throughout the whole kingdom of Ahasuerus—the people of Mordecai.* (NKJV)

Because of his position and power, Haman persuaded the king through deception to sign a decree that authorized the destruction of the Jews and the confiscation of their properties. This was going to be the genocide of the Jewish race.

The word Purim actually comes from the casting of the lots ("pur"), until the day was decided for the destruction of the Jews. Esther 3:13 says,

> *And the letters were sent by couriers into all the king's provinces, to destroy, to kill, and to annihilate all the Jews, both young and old, little children and women, in one day, on the thirteenth day of the twelfth month, which is the month of Adar, and to plunder their possessions.* (NKJV)

The stage was set for a final stroke that would wipe out the Jewish people once and for all, finally succeeding in aborting Elohim's plan of ultimate redemption through the biological seed of Abraham, Isaac, Jacob, and Ye'shua.

When Satan thinks that he has won or that he has succeeded in outwitting us and is poised to destroy us or our family, church, business, or whatever, HaShem always has His ace in the hole. Queen Esther was strategically positioned to thwart Haman's plans and destroy the enemy of the Jews. Listen to the words of Mordecai to his niece, Queen Esther, who had hidden her true identity:

> *Do not think in your heart that you will escape in the king's palace any more than all the other Jews. For if you remain completely silent at this time, relief and deliverance will arise for the Jews from another place, but you and your father's house will perish. Yet who knows whether you have come to the kingdom for such a time as this?* (Esther 4:13–14, NKJV)

Subsequently, Esther called for a time of fasting and prayer, then proceeded to set in place her strategy. You can read the story yourself in Esther 4:16–10:3; Haman is ultimately destroyed, the Jews are given the right to defend themselves and destroy their enemies, and Mordecai is exalted into Haman's position.

This powerful story speaks of the great deliverance of the Jews from extinction and annihilation. The feast of Purim is celebrated to commemorate this very dramatic deliverance.

> *So they called these days Purim, after the name Pur. Therefore, because of all the words of this letter, what they had seen concerning this matter, and what had happened*

to them, the Jews established and imposed it upon themselves and their descendants and all who would join them, that without fail they should celebrate these two days every year, according to the written instructions and according to the prescribed time, that these days should be remembered and kept throughout every generation, every family, every province, and every city, that these days of Purim should not fail to be observed among the Jews, and that the memory of them should not perish among their descendants. (Esther 9:26–28, NKJV)

Purim is distinct from all the other feasts, because it really focuses on a time of great celebration. The other feasts are more somber, reflective, and provoke a time of self-introspection, whereas this feast is purely a time for revelry and joy.

Observance of the Feast

Even though the feast focuses on the unrestrained joy of deliverance and the destruction of the enemy, it begins with a twenty-four-hour fast, recalling Queen Esther's call for a three-day fast prior to coming before the king. At the end of the fast, the celebration begins, accompanied by gifts being given to the poor and needy, according to Esther 9:22. It really is a time of great feasting. The general festive meal is called Seudat, and a party atmosphere sets in beginning at sunset, on the fourteenth day of the month of Adar; it continues through to the following day.

The second day is often called Shushan Purim, because the Jews celebrated for an extra day in Persia (see Esther 9:18). During this time of festivity, some distinctive traditions are observed for the purpose of teaching and reminding us of the past. The first tradition involves the eating of hamentashen cookies; these are triangular cookies stuffed with jam or another sweet filling. Hamentashen actually is a Yiddish word which means "Haman's pockets." Others call them "Haman's ears." The second distinct aspect of Purim is the reading of the scroll (Meggillat Esther) with a dramatic reenactment called a Purim spiel. As the scroll is read and Haman is mentioned, everyone boos with a loud voice. When Mordecai is mentioned, everyone shouts and cheers thunderously. Often children will dress up as Mordecai and Queen Esther, rejoicing for their great victory over Haman.

Ultimately there are two core principles conveyed in the feast. The first is the faithfulness of God. Obviously the story reminds us that God is a faithful God who will deliver us. When it seems that there is no way out, or that destruction is imminent, God is always faithful. The covenant blessings of provision, protection, and preservation confirm the faithfulness of God regarding His promises; He will keep and maintain His Word because He is a Covenant-keeping God, and we can rest assured that God will always keep His word to protect us when we cry out to him.

A point of interest in this story is that the name of God is not mentioned, but we see Him at work behind the scenes.

Every morning, I pray scriptures to God aloud, standing upon His promises. One of the scriptures I pray is Psalm 91, which reads:

He who dwells in the secret place of the Most High shall abide under the shadow of the Almighty. I will say of the Lord, "He is my refuge and my fortress; my God, in Him I will trust."

Surely He shall deliver you from the snare of the fowler And from the perilous pestilence. He shall cover you with His feathers, and under His wings you shall take refuge; His truth shall be your shield and buckler. You shall not be afraid of the terror by night, nor of the arrow that flies by day, nor of the pestilence that walks in darkness, nor of the destruction that lays waste at noonday.

A thousand may fall at your side, ad ten thousand at your right hand; but it shall not come near you. Only with your eyes shall you look, and see the reward of the wicked.

Because you have made the Lord, who is my refuge, even the Most High, your dwelling place, no evil shall befall you, nor shall any plague come near your dwelling; for He shall give His angels charge over you, to keep you in all your ways. In their hands they shall bear you up, lest you dash your foot against a stone. You shall tread upon the lion and the cobra, the young lion and the serpent you shall trample underfoot.

"Because he has set his love upon Me, therefore I will deliver him; I will set him on high, because he has known

My name. He shall call upon Me, and I will answer him; I will be with him in trouble; I will deliver him and honor him. With long life I will satisfy him, and show him My salvation." (NKJV)

This passage highlights the faithfulness of God to protect us from our enemies, calamities, and catastrophes. Even when it seems that we have been unfaithful, God always remains faithful to rescue us in time of trouble. What a great God we serve!

The second core principle conveys the responsibility of men to respond and act in accordance with the will of God. We forget often that God is waiting in every situation to see if we will step out, believe Him, and be willing to risk everything to do what is right! As in the case of Queen Esther, she was willing to expose her true identity as a Jewish woman. Adding to this, she was to present herself before the king, which was against protocol, risking her very life. This responsibility will continually be challenged in our private lives, as well as our public lives.

The feast of Purim, though considered a minor feast, is nonetheless significant in conveying strong principles for Jews and believing Gentiles.

Hanukkah
(The Feast of Dedication)

THE FEAST OF DEDICATION (HANNUKAH OR CHANNUKAH) IS not listed in Leviticus 23 with the other holy days, yet it is mentioned in the New Testament affirming that Jesus celebrated it at this time. We find the following recorded in John 10:22–23: *"Then came Hanukkah in Yerushalayim. It was winter, and Yeshua was walking around inside the Temple area, in Shlomo's Colonnade"* (CJB). Particularly this feast was established a couple of generations prior to the birth of Ye'shua during the time that historians and theologians refer to as the Intertestamental Period. It was a period of four hundred years between the ending of the Old Testament writings to the beginning of the New Testament era.

During this time, the Greek Empire under Alexander the Great succeeded in establishing Hellenism through conquest of the known world. After the untimely death of Alexander, the empire was divided into four quarters governed by his four generals. The Ptolomies took control of the south, and the Seleucids took control of the north;

eventually the Seleucids took control of Judea under the rulership of Antiochus IV, who adopted the title of "Epiphanies" (God manifest).

Conflicts and crises then began to emerge for devout Jews who refused to be assimilated into the culture of Hellenism. Antiochus viewed this refusal as rebellion and, not surprisingly, he began to enforce the policy of assimilation. In fact, an ultimatum was given to the Jews: either give up your distinctive observances of Shabbat, kosher laws, circumcision, etc. or face death. The Syrians under Antiochus marched in and defiled the golden Menorah, the utensils, the altars, and everything that was sacred to the Jewish people. Antiochus ordered a pig to be sacrificed on the holy altar and erected a statue of the Greek god Zeus in the temple, which obviously provoked the Jews beyond pacifism into outright confrontation! It was a turbulent time of uncertainty and trouble for the Jewish people.

In the midst of this trouble, a godly priest named Mattatias lived in the small village of Modi'in, and he had five sons. The Syrian soldiers were about to erect an idol and then force the inhabitants, the Jews, to eat pork and thus desecrate them once and for all. This provocation was the last straw, fueling a revolt led by the oldest son, Judah (nicknamed Maccabee, which means "the hammer").

Eventually the impossible happened: the Maccabees forced the Syrians out of Israel, recapturing Jerusalem as well. Then came the task of cleansing the temple that had been desecrated by the Syrians. The altars were cleansed, as well as the utensils, and especially the menorah. However, only one day's worth of purified oil was found to light the menorah, and it would take eight days to prepare more oil.

The following miracle is the reason Hanukkah is celebrated for eight days. The oil supernaturally lasted for eight days to keep the light of God burning until more oil was available. Thus the temple was restored to full function and rededicated to the God of Israel. An eight-day festival was established called Hanukkah (Hebrew for "dedication"). Every year, starting on the twenty-fifth day of Kislev, the Jewish community recalls the twofold miracle: the enduring oil and the miraculous military victory.

Observance of the Feast

As mentioned earlier, Hanukkah begins on the twenty-fifth day of Kislev at sunset with the lighting of the Hanukkiyah, the nine-branched Hanukkah menorah. The usual menorah has seven branches and thus is distinguished.

The eight branches remind us of the eight days of oil that burned miraculously, with the appropriate number of candles lit each day. The ninth branch, in the center of the menorah, is the candle that lights the others, and it is called the shamash (Hebrew for "servant"). During the festive meal, traditional songs are sung and the blessings recited. Because of the miracle of oil, it is customary to eat foods cooked in oil, such as latkes (potato pancakes) and sufganiot (Israeli doughnuts), recalling the miracle. More recently, it has become customary to give gifts to family members, and in many cases Hanukkah gelt (money) is given to children—twenty-five cents for every year of their age.

Obviously many make a comparison with the holiday of Christmas, but the purpose for these two festivals is different. One celebrates the birth of the Messiah; the other the deliverance of Israel from its oppressors. This festival can be very significant for Gentile believers in Ye'shua, however, because Ye'shua is the light of the world. As a family or church lights the appropriate candles of the Hannukiyah with the shamash candle, lighting the candles from right to left, prayers of thanksgiving for the Messiah's light can be given. Calls can be made for the Messiah to come. These unique times of lighting the candles offer a visual of the coming Messiah, the light of the world who will deliver His people from the tyranny of wicked oppressors.

During the lighting of the shamash and the appropriate number of candles, the following blessings are declared:

Baruch atah Adonai Elohenu melekh Ha'olam, Asher kidshanu b'mitzvohtav, v'tzi-vanu l'hadleck Ner, Shel Hanukkah.
(Blessed are You, O Lord our God, King of the universe, who has set us apart by Your commandments and commanded us to kindle the light of Hanukkah.)

And then it is added:

*Baruch atah Adonai Elohenu melekh ha-olam, she-asah
nisim l'avotenu, bayamim ha-hem, bazman hazeh.*
(Blessed are You, O Lord our God, King of the
universe, who has done miracles for our fathers in the
days at this season.)

On the first night only, these words are recited:

*Baruch ata Adonai Elohenu melekh ha'olam, she-he-
khiyanu vikiyamana vihigiyanu lazman hazeh.*
(Blessed are You, O Lord our God, King of the
universe who has kept us in life, sustained us, and
brought us to this season.)

After the lighting of the candles and reciting the blessings,
the family enjoys together a wonderful meal accompanied by
songs, laughter, and joyous conversation.

A final note to consider is that Jesus celebrated this festival
in the very temple that had been cleansed and restored two
generations prior to His coming. If Jesus is a model, there
is obviously no question about the validity of this feast of
dedication and its fruitful effect on Gentile believers.

Shabbat

I HAVE CHOSEN TO LEAVE THIS FESTIVE OBSERVANCE FOR THE
end, because this day is celebrated every seven days in a cyclical
way. God Himself modelled this observance and established
it for all men to follow, whether Jew or Gentile. However,
I believe that the Jewish understanding of Shabbat has a
deeper and greater significance than even most Christians
understand.

Consider the scriptures in Leviticus 23:1–3:

*And the Lord spoke to Moses, saying, "Speak to the children
of Israel, and say to them: 'The feasts of the Lord, which
you shall proclaim to be holy convocations, these are My
feasts. Six days shall work be done, but the seventh
day is a Sabbath of solemn rest, a holy convocation. You
shall do no work on it; it is the Sabbath of the Lord in all
your dwellings.'"* (NKJV)

I would like to draw your attention to the command the Lord gave to Israel, because in it we find the very reason for the observance of Shabbat (the Sabbath). Notice that God says that *"the seventh day is a Sabbath of solemn rest, a holy convocation."* The words "solemn rest" and "holy convocation" clearly convey to us the core values of the Sabbath. Let's consider them one at a time.

Solemn Rest

I do not think it is too difficult for anyone to fully comprehend the necessity of rest. This principle of rest encompasses every facet of our human existence. We all definitely need physical rest, or times of recuperation and recovery. Our bodies cannot sustain function and mobility without an opportunity to rest and recover. Energy, vitality, and mental clarity are restored when there is a healthy dosage of rest. Without adequate rest, there is a risk of physical, emotional, and mental breakdowns. Rest brings life and rejuvenation, and it is mandatory for longevity in life to continue.

Consider that God Himself, the omnipotent Creator, modelled for his creation the principles of rest. In Genesis 2:1–3, after God created for six days, we read,

> *Thus the heavens and the earth, and all the host of them, were finished. And on the seventh day God ended His work which He had done, and He rested on the seventh day from all His work which He had done. Then God*

blessed the seventh day and sanctified it, because in it He rested from all His work which God had created and made. (NKJV)

I want to draw your attention to the passage which says that God *"blessed the seventh day and sanctified it."* God did two things to establish the importance of rest: He blessed this day and sanctified it.

The significance of these two actions is great, but let's consider these two actions individually.

First of all, God blessed the day of rest. That is a powerful statement! In other words, the Lord delights in our rest and relaxation. That may seem difficult to accept as a concept, especially if one is driven by a religious mindset. Religion places a high priority on performance and duty. In fact, religious protocol emphasizes doing, busyness, and religious action. For one to simply do nothing but rest is considered by some a waste of time and productivity, yet God reserves a special blessing for His people on the seventh day of rest. I would venture to say that when we do not rest on the seventh day, we literally disqualify ourselves from God's blessing!

In our modern twenty-first-century society, with all its demands and time constraints, it seems increasingly difficult to simply stay put and rest. On our days off, we find opportunities to accomplish tasks or assignments that we could not do during our regular workweeks. Obviously someone may argue a justification for doing this, but that does not release the blessings of the Lord upon this day.

God makes it so clear that a blessing experienced only through the day of rest regenerates and restores our bodies, minds, and emotions. The absence of work truly releases a person to rest all their faculties, mentally and emotionally, and that will surely strengthen their body.

Secondly, God sanctified it. This action has all too often been misunderstood! The word "sanctify" does not only speak of something sacred; it speaks of designating value and uniqueness to an object, person, place, or day. To declare something sanctified literally means to set it apart for a specific purpose.

In the context of rest, the seventh day was specifically set aside to allow us to rest and recuperate. By sanctifying this day, the Lord clearly emphasized its value, significance, and uniqueness.

It follows six days of labor, work, or study, which takes a toll on our bodies, minds, and emotions. Whether one's vocation demands physical energy or intellectual property, the end result is the consumption of energy which leads to exhaustion. Stress-related jobs and positions in particular cause people to break down emotionally when this principle of the Sabbath rest is not followed. Therefore, the biblical precedent is unmistakable. It is there for the purpose of maintaining a sustainability and longevity to life.

Holy Convocation

The second description used to describe the observance of Shabbat are the words "holy convocation." Once again, the word holy conveys the principle of setting something apart for a specific purpose. The word convocation is very significant and must be rightly understood and applied if we are to access the blessing of God.

To convocate means to convene, to gather, to assemble collectively. This implies that an audience of one cannot be considered a convocation. This is significant because, unfortunately, a segment of society does not see the importance of convening in a church or synagogue, but in fact avoids places of worship altogether. I am not addressing the atheists or secularists who have no understanding or appreciation for houses of worship. Sadly, I am addressing so-called Christians and Jews who have embraced a watered down view of corporate worship! Even more disturbing are their bold claims that the church or synagogue can be experienced even in a Starbucks, with a latte in hand. I think we can safely say that we carry the presence of God in our lives wherever we go, but the commanded blessing of Shabbat is released through rest and a holy convocation in the house of the Lord (Adonai). King David expressed the longing of his heart in Psalm 27 by declaring,

> One thing I have desired of the Lord, that will I seek: that I may dwell in the house of the Lord all the days of my life, to behold the beauty of the Lord, and to inquire in His temple. For in the time of trouble He shall hide me in His pavilion; in the secret place of His tabernacle He shall hide me; He shall set me high upon a rock. And

now my head shall be lifted up above my enemies all around me; therefore I will offer sacrifices of joy in His tabernacle; I will sing, yes, I will sing praises to the Lord.
(Psalms 27:4–6, NKJV)

David's desire was to live in the house of the Lord, to visit in His temple all the days of His life. Why? Because he wanted to see the beauty of the Lord!

Now consider this: David knew that there is a beauty of the Lord that can only be seen and experienced in the setting of a holy convocation, an assembling of many worshippers. Yes, I can read your mind as the words come from your lips: "But God is everywhere!" This statement is accurate, but it *does* contradict what David is saying. Let's cut to the chase. Within the scope of science and development, there is the study of environmental conditioning and its impact on growth and development. Animal species and plant life, for example, have demonstrated this principle beautifully. Creation's ability to adapt and mutate to a certain environment proves without a shadow of doubt that environments create dynamics that are unique for a species' survival. Let me remind you that this is how God wanted it; He set in place the laws and they are unmistakable.

In light of what has just been shared, a holy convocation in the house of the Lord creates a dynamic that allows the participants to see the beauty of the Lord in a unique way! Corporate worship and prayer can have the same effect that a bonfire has upon people. A twig on fire can easily be consumed and the fire goes out. But when many twigs and logs are amassed together, the fire grows in strength and sustainability! I don't know anyone who doesn't like to be gathered around a huge bonfire at night to enjoy the colors, crackling, and warmth of that fire.

Right from the beginning of creation, humanity understood the necessity of a bonfire and its effectiveness for our survival. If you travel to some of the most remote and primeval civilizations in the world, you will still find them gathering around tribal fires for the purpose of social interaction and communication. The passing down of oral traditions and telling of stories from one generation to the next is still a central part of the tribes' survival and sustainability. Convocation, in the broadest sense, is critical and significant, for it provides an experience that is beneficial and contributes to the individual and to social harmony.

A Shabbat for Adonai

The third description used for the observance of Shabbat can be found in these words: "It is for the Lord." I think that our human reasoning often focuses on the benefit that an activity, product, or event offers before engaging ourselves. That is human nature. Even though the purpose of observing Shabbat clearly benefits our bodies, minds, and quality of life, the prime purpose of Shabbat is directed towards honoring the Lord.

When we honor the Sabbath by not doing our own things, or pursuing tasks or assignments that do not include

God in their purpose, the Lord is pleased. When we choose to honor the Lord by spending time in His house of worship, with His family, and then choosing to spend time with our biological families, we delight His heart. The observance of Shabbat is an individual and corporate experience. I would, in fact, make this statement regarding the command to honor Shabbat: to fully observe the requirements of this mitzvah (imperative), we must engage in corporate family worship and individual corporal rest. Let me repeat that equation for you this way:

corporate worship + corporal rest = Shabbat

Without these two components, a person is not observing Shabbat biblically and spiritually. Consider what the Apostle Paul declares to the Hebrew believers in Ye'shua about the importance of corporate worship:

And let us consider one another in order to stir up love and good works, not forsaking the assembling of ourselves together, as is the manner of some, but exhorting one another, and so much the more as you see the Day approaching. (Hebrews 10:24–25, NKJV)

Let's unpack these two verses in an expositional way so that we can better understand this admonition and warning. Notice that we are to *"consider one another in order to stir up love and good works."* The very nature of these words demands that we engage in a corporate setting, encouraging each other by gathering together in our congregational meetings. The expression of love and good works is displayed in a corporate setting through the encouragement of all participants. A person may say that they love the family of God, but if he refuses to engage in a corporate, congregational meeting, he is deceiving himself. In fact, I would venture to say that the enemy has succeeded in thwarting that believer's true identity, rendering him spiritually impotent!

Many individuals who promote this kind of thinking are really hiding their true motivation, which is to be free of any accountability. Let's be honest and clear regarding this issue. When someone separates himself from his family, the reason is to pursue independence, not wanting to give account for his actions. At the root of this thinking is a spirit of rebellion masked in the guise of maturity and being one's own man. However, corporate worship is the vehicle of observing Shabbat for the Lord, coming into His house to be with Him and His family.

Secondly, I want to draw your attention to the latter part of Hebrews 10:25, which says, *"...but exhorting one another, and so much the more as you see the Day approaching."* Why should we encourage others? Because the Day is approaching!

The reference to the approaching day is very significant. In the Scriptures, you will frequently find the expression "the day of the Lord." This phrase speaks of the day of the outpouring of God's wrath upon sinful men, societies, and cities. It would seem that we have entered the season of the end. Biblical prophecy is being fulfilled right before our eyes as nations align, positioning themselves, even though they are not aware of it, to fulfill the end-time purposes of God. Specifically, the Middle East and Europe are highlighted to be key players in the final outcome of God's plan to establish the one new man. In fact, the nations of these two regions will find themselves directly engaged in a relationship with Israel and the unfolding of God's plan. I personally believe that the parable of the sheep and the goats in Matthew 25:31–46 refers to nations and their response to Israel.

Let's now take a closer look at these scriptures and dig out some nuggets of truth.

The Sheep and the Goats (Matthew 25:31–46)

When the Son of Man comes in His glory, and all the holy angels with Him, then He will sit on the throne of His glory. All the nations will be gathered before Him, and He will separate them one from another, as a shepherd divides his sheep from the goats. And He will set the sheep on His right hand, but the goats on the left. Then the King will say to those on His right hand, "Come, you blessed of My Father, inherit the kingdom prepared for you from the foundation of the world: for I was hungry and you gave Me food; I was thirsty and you gave Me drink; I was a stranger and you took Me in; I was naked and you clothed Me; I was sick and you visited Me; I was in prison and you came to Me."

Then the righteous will answer Him, saying, "Lord, when did we see You hungry and feed You, or thirsty and give You drink? When did we see You a stranger and take You in, or naked and clothe You? Or when did we see You sick, or in prison, and come to You?" And the King will answer and say to them, "Assuredly, I say to you, inasmuch as you did it to one of the least of these My brethren, you did it to Me."

Then He will also say to those on the left hand, "Depart from Me, you cursed, into the everlasting fire prepared for the devil and his angels: for I was hungry and you gave Me no food; I was thirsty and you gave Me no drink; I was a stranger and you did not take Me in, naked and you did not clothe Me, sick and in prison and you did not visit Me."

Then they also will answer Him, saying, "Lord, when did we see You hungry or thirsty or a stranger or naked or sick or in prison, and did not minister to You?" Then He will answer them, saying, "Assuredly, I say to you, inasmuch as you did not do it to one of the least of these, you did not do it to Me." And these will go away into everlasting punishment, but the righteous into eternal life." (Matthew 25:31–46, NKJV)

Jesus then addresses those on His left, the goats, the ones who did the opposite, not feeding or clothing themselves. He cursed them—or more correctly, referred to them—saying, *"Depart from Me, you cursed, into the everlasting fire prepared for the devil and his angels"* (Matthew 25:41, NKJV). This portion of Scripture concludes in Matthew 25:46, which says, *"And these will go away into everlasting punishment, but the righteous into eternal life"* (NKJV).

Exegesis: The Art of Interpretation

When we seek to understand and rightly discern Scripture, certain interpreting principles must be applied. These principles are known as exegesis, a Greek word that simply means "the art of interpretation."

When we seek to understand Scripture, we must begin by asking the text a number of questions which will allow us to discover and discern rightly. To better understand the significance and interpretation of a scripture, we must look at it through two specific lenses: the grammatical and the historical.

When we speak of the grammatical lens, we are referring to the study of specific words and their root meanings. The art of word study is called etymology; to research root meanings is to pursue on etymological study.

The historical lens focuses on an understanding of the cultural, environmental, and social context of the historical period in question. Once we have a knowledge of the historical period, we have a better understanding of the perception and reception of the readership. For example, if you were to take the word "gay" to describe someone in 1925 England, it would simply mean someone who is a jolly, happy fellow. However, the same word today describes and identifies someone who pursues a homosexual lifestyle. Therefore, the time period—culturally, socially, and environmentally—does play a significant part in rightly interpreting Scripture, or for that matter any literature.

Going back to the story of the sheep and the goats in Matthew 25:31–46, we need to ask questions like these:

- To whom was the story addressed?
- What was the context of the conversation?
- What was the theme of the conversation?
- What was the general environment and social situation of the day?

The answer to these four questions will truly help us understand and rightly interpret the story and determine what Jesus was saying. We must also focus our attention on specific words that reveal the greater significance.

A closer examination of this passage will reveal that the context is totally Jewish. When Ye'shua came, He clearly identified that His mission was to the lost sheep of Israel. When the Messiah came, He did not travel out of Israel, nor did He go into Gentile-populated cities. He chose to minister within Israel and to the Jewish people.

The concept of the church as the ecclesia, the formation of a living organism upon the earth (the body of Christ) was inaugurated after the death, resurrection, and ascension of Ye'shua to heaven. He commanded His disciples to go and wait in Yerushalayim for the promise of the Father, the coming of the Holy Spirit. Notice what He said:

He commanded them not to depart from Jerusalem, but to wait for the Promise of the Father, "which," He said, "you have heard from Me; for John truly baptized with water, but you shall be baptized with the Holy Spirit not many days from now." (Acts 1:4–5, NKJV)

Ye'shua continued in Acts 1:8:

But you shall receive power when the Holy Spirit has come upon you; and you shall be witnesses to Me in Jerusalem, and in all Judea and Samaria, and to the end of the earth. (NKJV)

The imperative was for them to wait and be empowered to become witnesses and thus fulfill the great commission. Ye'shua definitely did not have the church in mind when He spoke the story of the sheep and the goats. Consider as well that the scripture declares that the nations (*ethnos*, a Greek word to describe the ethnic designations of the world) were gathered around the throne, and He separated them as a shepherd would separate sheep from goats. It did not refer to people from the beginning of time to the present, but rather nations presenting themselves; the language is corporate.

Now consider the words of Jesus: *"Assuredly, I say to you, inasmuch as you did it to one of the least of these My brethren, you did it to Me"* (NKJV). Once again, Ye'shua was a Jew and His mission was to the Jewish people. Therefore, it is very clear that He was speaking of the biological descendants of Abraham. The replacement theologian would interpret this scripture to refer to Christians. However, Jesus was speaking to a Jewish crowd in the context of Israel being the least of nations; the scripture speaks about the judgment of nations and how they treat Israel. If nations will help and bless Israel in their time of need, they will be considered "sheep nations."

I believe the parallel is very simple: sheep are docile and provide milk, fleece, and even their meat to feed and sustain Israel. The goats represent the unruly and rebellious head-butting nations that will not help Israel. They will incur upon themselves the curse. These goat nations will be clearly identified by their treatment of Israel.

When Elohim called out Avram Avinu from the Chaldeans, He set in place a principle of sowing and reaping regarding His descendants. In Genesis 12:2–3, we read,

> *I will make you a great nation; I will bless you and make your name great; and you shall be a blessing. I will bless those who bless you, and I will curse him who curses you; and in you all the families of the earth shall be blessed."* (NKJV)

This principle is displayed in the story of the sheep and the goats, those who will be blessed and those who will be cursed! Therefore, the nations of the world are even now being positioned to fulfill biblical prophecy and contribute to the ultimate plan of God, the establishment of the one new man.

The day of the Lord is fast approaching and nations hang in the balance.

Let's take a closer look at the traditional observance of Shabbat in a Jewish home. The command to observe Shabbat comes from Exodus 20:8: *"Remember the Sabbath day, to keep it holy"* (NKJV). The twofold theme is simply to remember the Creator and set aside a day to rest in Him.

The preparation for Shabbat is a very special time. On Friday afternoons, the mother of the house brings out her finest linen and silverware to decorate the dinner table and cook the finest meal of the week to commemorate this holy day. Two candlesticks are placed on the table to remind everyone of the theme: to remember and sanctify this day. According to rabbinic tradition, the women of the house must light the candles eighteen minutes before the commencement of Shabbat at sundown, and then declare a blessing over the lights with a circling of her arms to draw the light to herself. Once she has done this, she recites these words of blessing:

Baruch Atah Adonai ELohenu melekh ha-olam, asher Kidshanu b'mitzvohtav v'tzi-vanu l'hadleek Ner shel Shabbat.
(Blessed are You, Lord our God, King of the universe, who has set us apart by Your commandments and has commanded us to kindle the Sabbath lights.)

The woman closes her eyes and offers a silent prayer, and when she opens her eyes, according to rabbinic teaching,

Shabbat has officially begun. The man of the house then raises the cup of wine to offer a blessing to the family. This is the Kiddush cup, the cup of sanctification. He recites this blessing:

Barukh'atah Adonai Elohenu melekh ha-olam, boray p'ree hagahfen.
(Blessed are You, Lord our God, King of the universe, who creates the fruit of the vine.)

Next comes the blessing over the challah, the trusted egg bread which is traditionally used for Shabbat. Generally speaking, two loaves represent the double portion of manna in the desert. The bread is covered with a beautiful white cloth on a decorative challah plate. The man of the house, or leader, then speaks the blessing over the bread, declaring,

Barukh atah Adonai Eloheinu melek ha-olam, ha-motzee lekhem meen ha-aretz.
(Blessed are you Lord our God, King of the universe, who brings forth bread from the earth.)

The bread is then broken by hand and passed around and salted to symbolize the salt on the sacrifices in the temple era. No knife is to be used, to symbolize the day when the Messiah comes and all weapons of war will be done away with. As they eat the bread, the greeting of Shabbat Shalom (Peaceful Sabbath) are exchanged with hugs and kisses. A final prayer and blessing are then given by the father over his children; he begins by placing his right hand over the head of his son, and says,

> *Y'simkh a elohim K'ephrayeem v'khee M'nasheh.*
> (May God make you like Ephraim and Manasseh.)[4]

For his daughters he gives them this blessing,

> *Y'simekh elohim k'Sarah, Rivkah, rakhel v'Leah.*
> (May you be like Sarah, Rebekah, Rachel, and Leah.)

The father turns to his wife and, as a husband, blesses her by reciting the Aishet Khayeel (the passage of the virtuous woman from Proverbs 31:10–31).

Once the blessings are recited, the meal is served and the family enjoys an evening of food fellowship and fun. As you can imagine, the conversation around the table is lively, and at times provocative. Children will ask questions about the Torah or life in general. The older ones engage in heated debates, quoting the sages and rabbinical sources, and all of this contributes to healthy family relationships and cohesiveness.

Consider the impact of Shabbat through the centuries, as Jewish people in the Diaspora sustained their identity despite immense pressure to lose themselves in assimilation to the cultures and nations where they lived and were born. Truly Shabbat and its observance can be considered the most

---

[4] See Genesis 48:20.

significant anchor of identity for the Jewish people. Through the centuries, persecution and intermarriage did force many Jews to fully assimilate and embrace the identities of their homeland nations. The result was that they would not openly observe or remember and sanctify Shabbat, for fear of being labeled and ostracized. However, one can never fully deny one's roots and lineage.

The eve of Shabbat is observed and celebrated with the family, but in the morning the family makes its way to a special celebration or service for Shabbat at their synagogue or church. The Shabbat service involves a reading and study of the weekly Torah. The focus is on preaching and teaching the weekly portions of Scripture, or a variety of other topics that build up the body. Obviously, worship and celebration are very much part of the Shabbat service. As you can imagine, a number of different variations can be implemented to render the weekly experience of Shabbat enjoyable and significant.

Every family or congregation can learn a simple song entitled "Shabbat Shalom," a song that declares, "May you experience the peace of Shabbat."

Conclusion

The weekly celebration of Shabbat for an individual family or congregation serves as a reminder to honor God and family. One's need for rest brings great benefits—spiritually, emotionally, socially, and physically. God's ways are perfect and complete. The Creator who created us knows full well what is required for our mental, emotional, physical, and spiritual health. When we follow His mitzvahs (the commands and clear instructions in His Word) we will prosper in every way. Consider what the psalmist declares:

> *Blessed are the undefiled in the way, who walk in the law of the Lord! Blessed are those who keep His testimonies, who seek Him with the whole heart! They also do no iniquity; they walk in His ways. You have commanded us to keep Your precepts diligently. Oh, that my ways were directed to keep Your statutes! Then I would not be ashamed, when I look into all Your commandments.* (Psalm 119:1–6, NKJV)

Did you notice that true happiness is reserved for those who walk and live according to the Word of the Lord? The psalmist continues,

> *Your word I have hidden in my heart, that I might not sin against You. Blessed are You, O Lord! Teach me Your statutes. With my lips I have declared all the judgments of Your mouth. I have rejoiced in the way of Your testimonies, as much as in all riches. I will meditate on Your precepts, and contemplate Your ways. I will delight myself in Your statutes; I will not forget Your word. Deal bountifully with Your servant, that I may live and keep Your word. Open my eyes, that I may see wondrous things from Your law.* (Psalm 119:11–18, NKJV)

I believe that observing and celebrating Shabbat and all the feasts will truly enrich Gentile believers and churches. If believers in Ye'shua will treasure, delight in, and not forget the instructions of the Word of God, His precepts, and His regulations, the Lord will deal generously with His servants.

It is clear to me that many in the Christian church are being deprived of the wealth and blessing of applying the Word of God from a Jewish context, and the reason is simple ignorance. Many leaders in the body of Christ are sadly deceived, thinking that Christianity only finds its roots in the New Testament. In so thinking, they subconsciously place very little value and relevance on the Tanach, the Old Testament; they will not deny its inspiration and authenticity, but subtly downplay its relevance. This specific lens, when applied, causes a person to work with only part of the equation, which inevitably leads to theological confusion and misrepresentation.

As I mentioned earlier, a student of the Bible will be impoverished because they will not even look for the hidden treasure found in the Tanach because of their disassociation from Jewish roots.

13

Prayer, the Prayer Shawl, and the Shofar

A VERY SIGNIFICANT TOOL FOR PRAYER IS THE USE OF THE TALLIT, the prayer shawl, in daily prayer and fellowship with God. Sadly, many have not been able to experience the effectiveness of prayer and intimacy with God on a deeper level because of ignorance and misunderstanding of this subject. I believe a proper understanding and usage of a tallit can be significant and meaningful in prayer.

I would like to begin by stating that Jesus and the disciples did not wear a tallit as we see today, but instead wore a cloak (or mantle) with the tassels (or fringes) on the four corners, as was commanded by HaShem to remember all the mitzvahs (the commandments of the Lord). I would also want to clarify that the tallit serves only as a memorial of the cloak that the Jewish men wore in that day, to which the tzitzit were attached.

The tallit was established later on as a Jewish observance and practice, but once again I must emphatically state that Ye'shua did not wear a tallit. Please keep this in mind as we consider the usage and contemporary practice of the prayer shawl.

In a North American twenty-first century setting, men do not wear robes but pants and shirts. As I mentioned earlier, some very observant Jews choose to wear a vest with tassels (tallit katan) and others simply tied tassels to their belts to fulfill this requirement. The point, very simply, is that the prayer shawl with tassels can be a blessing in modelling Jesus during times of prayer as a point of contact with spiritual significance. I will address this truth in detail further on.

As we consider the significance of the tallit and the tzitzit, and how they can function as a blessing in your prayer life, keep in mind that your first reaction to this truth should not be "You are being religious and legalistic." If Jesus is our model, and He wore the tzitzit, then could it be that we are missing something that could enrich our lives?

As I share the scriptures and concepts of the tallit, I encourage you to study and meditate on them and ask yourself this question: have you been in the dark so long regarding the Jewishness of Jesus—or even worse, have you possibly been influenced by a religious spirit that has prevailed through Christendom, which has tainted your view? If you have not considered the authenticity of the Jewishness of the Bible, then I ask you to please consider the possibility that Christian tradition has become a lens that colors your perception and practices.

The Jewish Perspective of Wearing the Tallit

In Numbers 15:37–40, the Lord commands the people,

> *Tell them to make tassels on the corners of their garments throughout their generations, and to put a blue thread in the tassels of the corners. And you shall have the tassel, that you may look upon it and remember all the commandments of the Lord and do them, and that you may not follow the harlotry to which your own heart and your own eyes are inclined, and that you may remember and do all My commandments, and be holy for your God.* (NKJV)

Deuteronomy 22:12, states, *"You shall make tassels on the four corners of the clothing with which you cover yourself"* (NKJV). These two scriptures clearly describe the purpose of the tzitzit, the tassels or fringes on the garments that remind the wearer of all the commandments of the Lord.

The tzitzit, eight in total, remind us of the 613 laws of the Torah, the dos and don'ts, so to speak. There are 248 positive commands (the dos) and 365 negative commands (the don'ts). Consider that each Hebrew letter in the Hebrew alphabet has a corresponding numerical value. The numerical value of the five letters that comprise the word tzitzit add up to six hundred and the eight strings and five knots of each tassel equal thirteen, and thus we have 613 laws according to the Talmud. To list the laws here is not necessary, but you can find them listed by the great Rabbi Maimonides (the Rambam) in his work, the Mishneh Torah.

The emphasis is clearly on the tzitzit and not the garment or the shawl. It is believed that the word tallit is connected to the Latin word stola, which simply refers to a robe or cloak. The tallit was established later by rabbinical Judaism as a memorial for Jewish men to wear fringes on the four corners of their garments. Jesus did not wear a prayer shawl, but he wore a mantle with the fringes attached to the corners of his garment to fulfill the Law. I believe this must be clear for every Gentile believer that desires to emulate the Master, our High Priest, the Cohen Gadol, our heavenly Intercessor.

Now, there are different views regarding the spiritual significance of the tallit presented by Religious Jews. One view says that the tallit is a metaphor for God's infinite, transcendent light, and the tzitzit tassels allude to the imminent divine light which permeates every element of creation. According to some sects of Judaism, when the tallit gadol (the prayer shawl) or the tallit katan (the vest with tassels) is worn by men, it declares that the wearer is embracing the light of God and seeking to manifest that light in every area of his life.

Many tzitzits and tallits include a blue tassel (techelet). The dye of blue comes from the blood of a rare Mediterranean shellfish called the chilazon. Some rabbis do not wear the blue tassel, because they believe that the blue tassel will only be legitimate when the Messiah comes. Once again you see the positions and convictions embraced by different streams within Judaism. However, it is paramount that Gentile believers do not take lightly the usage of the tallit, creating a cause of offence to observant Jews, who only use the tallit at specific times.

I must also make a clear statement regarding women using a tallit in prayer. First of all, only men are permitted to pray with a tallit in public. For a women to wear a tallit in public worship, in the presence of observant Jewish men, is inappropriate and can be offensive. However, I believe a women can pray in private with a tallit, and it will be very significant, as we will expound further on.

For men considering the command more closely, the tallit is to be worn during the day when the tzitzit is visible, so that it reminds one of the mitzvot (commands) of the Lord. It must be worn during morning prayers and specifically in the service at night during Yom Kippur, the Day of Atonement (the Kol Nidrei).

The blessing that is recited before one places the tallit over their shoulder is very significant:

Blessed art thou, Lord our God, King of the universe, who has sanctified us by His commandments and has commanded us to wrap ourselves with the tzitzit.

According to Orthodox Jews who are very strict in their observance, when they put on their tallit to pray, they will recite these words:

I am wrapping myself in the Tzitzit, fulfilling the command of my creator as it is written in the Torah: they shall make them a Tzitzit upon the corners of the garments throughout their generations. And even as I cover myself with the Tallit in this world, so my soul will be clothed with a beautiful spiritual robe in the world to come, in the Garden of Eden.

Therefore, wearing a tallit as part of one's worship is central to observant Jews.

The Spiritual Significance for Believers

As we begin to consider the significance of the tallit during times of prayer, it's important to remind you again that Jesus, the disciples, and Jewish believers wore tassels or fringes on the four corners of their garment or mantle. They did not wear a prayer shawl, because that was a later tradition developed to remind observant Jews of the mitzvah to attach tassels to their cloaks. This does not mean that Gentile Believers cannot use a prayer shawl today in prayer, but it is imperative to not confuse biblical and historical truth with human tradition.

Using a prayer shawl wisely and appropriately can be a wonderful blessing to your spiritual life. Having said that, I will look at a number of scriptures that reveal and release insight that I believe will enrich your prayer life.

Luke 8 contains the story of a woman who was very sick, hemorrhaging blood for twelve years. She touched

Jesus and was healed. This is probably one of the most well-known miracles spoken about in sermons. We all admire the faith, determination, and humility of this woman who had exhausted all her resources trying to get well. And of course we remember the response of Ye'shua to this event. However, if you take a closer look at the details of this episode, you will find one of the most powerful truths regarding the tzitzit and its significance.

Now a woman, having a flow of blood for twelve years, who had spent all her livelihood on physicians and could not be healed by any, came from behind and touched the border of His garment. And immediately her flow of blood stopped.

And Jesus said, "Who touched Me?"

When all denied it, Peter and those with him said, "Master, the multitudes throng and press You, and You say, 'Who touched Me?'"

But Jesus said, "Somebody touched Me, for I perceived power going out from Me." Now when the woman saw that she was not hidden, she came trembling; and falling down before Him, she declared to Him in the presence of all the people the reason she had touched Him and how she was healed immediately.

And He said to her, "Daughter, be of good cheer; your faith has made you well. Go in peace." (Luke 8:43–48, NKJV)

The account in the Gospel of Mark says that she had said to herself, knowing that Ye'shua was coming, *"If only I may touch His clothes, I shall be made well"* (Mark 5:28, NKJV). Her declaration of faith prepared her for the release of a miracle. She activated her faith through the words "I shall be made well." I believe this woman confirms a powerful spiritual truth.

The power of our faith expressed through a declaration is a necessary ingredient to receiving a supernatural healing from the Lord. If we desire to receive from the Lord, the answer to all of our needs, this same principle of declaration must be exercised. Many scriptures reveal that great authority is released when we *say* as opposed to just *pray*.

What do I mean by that? The answer is very simple: there is a difference between presenting your need to God as a petition and addressing your need by declaring what God's Word says. In prayer, one approaches the Lord asking if a miracle is possible regarding a situation or need, whereas when you declare what the Word says about your situation, your approach comes in a tone of faith and assurance that God will intervene on your behalf.

> *For He Himself has said, "I will never Leave you nor forsake you." So we may boldly say: "The Lord is my helper; I will not fear. What can man do to me?"* (Hebrews 13:5–6, NKJV)

In this scripture, a precedent is being set. Because the Lord has said it, I can declare it with absolute boldness and assurance.

Another example comes in the Gospel of Mark, where Jesus speaks to His disciples about a withered fig tree that He had cursed the day before. He says the following about the authority of declaring God's Word:

> *So Jesus answered and said to them, "Have faith in God. For assuredly, I say to you, whoever says to this mountain, 'Be removed and be cast into the sea,' and does not doubt in his heart, but believes that those things he says will be done, he will have whatever he says."* (Mark 11:22–23, NKJV)

Very clearly, Ye'shua is teaching us a powerful tool of faith in action. You have the authority to declare God's words, and they have power to effect a change. When Jesus says "Have faith in God," this is actually translated in the original Greek as "Have God's kind of faith." In Genesis 1, God spoke the world and all of creation into existence by the power of His words. His words have creative power. Whatever God says will come to pass. Every promise in the Word is true and has power to manifest in our physical realm.

The life of Abraham clearly presents a confirmation of this principle, that faith in what God says will override and supersede even the natural laws and limitations of the physical world and all its impossibilities. The Apostle Paul, writing to the church in Rome, speaks of Abraham's faith this way:

Therefore it is of faith that it might be according to grace, so that the promise might be sure to all the seed, not only to those who are of the law, but also to those who are of the faith of Abraham, who is the father of us all (as it is written, "I have made you a father of many nations") in the presence of Him whom he believed—God, who gives life to the dead and calls those things which do not exist as though they did; who, contrary to hope, in hope believed, so that he became the father of many nations, according to what was spoken, "So shall your descendants be." And not being weak in faith, he did not consider his own body, already dead (since he was about a hundred years old), and the deadness of Sarah's womb. He did not waver at the promise of God through unbelief, but was strengthened in faith, giving glory to God, and being fully convinced that what He had promised He was also able to perform. And therefore "it was accounted to him for righteousness."

Now it was not written for his sake alone that it was imputed to him, but also for us. It shall be imputed to us who believe in Him who raised up Jesus our Lord from the dead... (Romans 4:16–24, NKJV)

This is one of the clearest declarations of the spiritual principle that faith in God's Word and promises will supersede even the natural laws of physical limitation. What may seem impossible for man is possible with God.

In context, Abraham received a clear promise from Adonai that he would be the father of many nations and that his descendants would be as numerous as the sand on the seashore and the stars in the sky. However, at the age of one hundred, he still did not have a child with Sarah, who was about ninety years old at this time. The natural laws of life and procreation dictate that they had now entered a season of their lives where procreation was impossible. We know that Sarah had already resigned herself to the fact that she would no longer be able to have children. When the Lord and two angels visited them prior to God making his decision to destroy Sodom and Gomorrah in Genesis 18:1–15, the encounter and subsequent conversation clearly revealed that Abraham believed what was being said to him, but Sarah had a difficult time believing. Her reaction of laughter, and then consequently denying that she had laughed, is an indicator that her first reaction was a reflection of deferred hope. She had a sense of disillusionment because she had physically passed beyond her childbearing years.

It is human and perfectly natural to focus on our present circumstances and lose sight of what God has said. The battle is very tense between faith in God's Word and the facts of our circumstances. If we succeed in embracing the truth with absolute conviction, our eyes will be fixed on God and not the facts. In essence, it really is all about our perspective.

I remember a story I heard many years ago about two prisoners who gathered around their window one evening. One looked down and saw the mud, but the other looked up and saw the stars. Their circumstance was the same; they were both in prison—but where they chose to fix their eyes determined what they saw. In the same way, the Scriptures declare that we walk by faith, not by sight. Our lives must be led by faith in God and His Word, and not by our natural reasoning mind.

Consider this defining moment for Abraham and Sarah:

Then the Lord appeared to him by the terebinth trees of Mamre, as he was sitting in the tent door in the heat of the day. So he lifted his eyes and looked, and behold, three men were standing by him; and when he saw them, he ran from the tent door to meet them, and bowed himself to the ground, and said, "My Lord, if I have now found favor in Your sight, do not pass on by Your servant. Please let a little water be brought, and wash your feet, and rest yourselves under the tree. And I will bring a morsel of bread, that you may refresh your hearts. After that you may pass by, inasmuch as you have come to your servant."

They said, "Do as you have said."

So Abraham hurried into the tent to Sarah and said, "Quickly, make ready three measures of fine meal; knead it and make cakes." And Abraham ran to the herd, took a tender and good calf, gave it to a young man, and he hastened to prepare it. So he took butter and milk and the calf which he had prepared, and set it before them; and he stood by them under the tree as they ate.

Then they said to him, "Where is Sarah your wife?"

So he said, "Here, in the tent."

And He said, "I will certainly return to you according to the time of life, and behold, Sarah your wife shall have a son."

(Sarah was listening in the tent door which was behind him.) Now Abraham and Sarah were old, well advanced in age; and Sarah had passed the age of childbearing. Therefore Sarah laughed within herself, saying, "After I have grown old, shall I have pleasure, my lord being old also?"

And the Lord said to Abraham, "Why did Sarah laugh, saying, 'Shall I surely bear a child, since I am old?' Is anything too hard for the Lord? At the appointed time I will return to you, according to the time of life, and Sarah shall have a son."

But Sarah denied it, saying, "I did not laugh," for she was afraid.

And He said, "No, but you did laugh!" (Genesis 18:1–15, NKJV)

What an amazing encounter for Abraham and Sarah. When they least expected it and when possibly all hope was gone, the Lord showed up and renewed His promise.

In Romans 4, we witness Abraham's faith in God regardless of natural impossibilities. The Bible says that He believed in One

who gives life to the dead and calls those things which do not exist as though they did... And not being weak in faith, he did not consider his own body, already dead (since he was about a hundred years old), and the deadness of Sarah's womb. He did not waver at the promise of God through unbelief, but was strengthened in faith, giving glory to God, and being fully convinced that what He had promised He was also able to perform. (Romans 4:17, 19–21, NKJV)

Notice that Abraham was fully convinced that God was able to do the impossible, and he did not allow his present situation to shake his belief in God's promise.

There is a phrase that has helped me personally through the years when I've found myself caught in the tension between the truth and the facts of my life. It says, "What you focus on, you make room for; and what you fear, you will empower." Friends, choose to believe God's truth and you will never be disappointed. Speak to your mountains the Word of God and you will see them removed out of your way.

Returning to the woman with the issue of blood, in our initial text she specifically purposed to touch the border of His garment—in truth, His tzitzit. This may seem insignificant to a Gentile believer who does not understand the historical Jewish practice of wearing the tzitzit, but to a Jew it is very significant. I would suggest to you that the tzitzit could represent the wings of the Lord. I will now share a number of scriptures that speak of the wings of the Lord, which carry great significance:

1. "But to you who fear My name the Sun of Righteousness shall arise with healing in His wings; and you shall go out and grow fat like stall-fed calves. You shall trample the wicked, for they shall be ashes under the soles of your feet on the day that I do this," says the Lord of hosts.

"Remember the Law of Moses, My servant, which I commanded him in Horeb for all Israel, with the statutes and judgments." (Malachi 4:2–4, NKJV)

2. He who dwells in the secret place of the Most High shall abide under the shadow of the Almighty. I will say of the Lord, "He is my refuge and my fortress; My God, in Him I will trust."

Surely He shall deliver you from the snare of the fowler and from the perilous pestilence. He shall cover you with His feathers, and under His wings you shall take refuge; His truth shall be your shield and buckler. (Psalms 91:1–4, NKJV)

3. And after Boaz had eaten and drunk, and his heart was cheerful, he went to lie down at the end of the heap of grain; and she came softly, uncovered his feet, and lay down.

Now it happened at midnight that the man was startled, and turned himself; and there, a woman was lying at his feet. And he said, "Who are you?"

*So she answered, "I am Ruth, your maidservant.
Take your maidservant under your wing, for you are a
close relative."* (Ruth 3:7–9 NKJV)

In these three scriptures, we find a powerful revelation
that can revitalize our spiritual lives. The prophet Malichi
describes the Lord as *"the Sun of Righteousness… with healing
in His wings"* (Malachi 4:2, NKJV). David declares that
under his wings we will find refuge, safety, and protection.
Consider this thought: one of the Hebrew connotations for
the word tassels (or fringes) is specifically the word "wings."

Now, when we wrap ourselves in the tallit, we are
spiritually coming under the wings of the Lord, experiencing
his refuge, peace, and protection. The use of the tallit in prayer
as one holds the tassels is to prophetically declare, "Lord, I
choose to come and access my healing by faith because you
said that the Sun of Righteousness has arisen with healing in
His wings. What a powerful vision and promise that we can
avail ourselves of! Hallelujah !

A second thought I would like to suggest to you is that
when we physically cover ourselves with the tallit, we are
spiritually choosing to come into the secret place of intimacy
with the Lord, according to Psalms 91:1: *"He who dwells in
the secret place of the Most High shall abide under the shadow of
the Almighty"* (NKJV).

In a physical sense, the wings of an eagle serve as a
protection for the eaglets from inclement weather, as well as
shade from the heat of the sun. The metaphor is powerful.

When I have been in times of trouble or anguish, I have prayed with my tallit, creating a secret place with God, and His presence soothes my soul and comforts me. Often in that place of covering my head with the tallit, the Lord speaks to me, giving me wisdom and understanding at the crossroads experiences of my life. I have felt Adonai's presence so close to me, like a mother eagle who shelters her eaglets in some of the most difficult times of life.

Covering my head with the tallit also reminds me of a Jewish wedding performed under a *chuppa*, which in its simplest form is a prayer shawl attached to four poles, held up by four men, forming a tent or covering over the couple. When we come into that secret place, symbolically creating our own little tent of meeting with God, we are able to focus and engage in prayer more easily. We enter into a covenant relationship of love with our Lord, the heavenly Bridegroom.

Another parallel I would like to make is the principle of putting on Christ, as the Word of God declares in Romans 13:12–14:

> *The night is far spent, the day is at hand. Therefore let us cast off the works of darkness, and let us put on the armor of light. Let us walk properly, as in the day, not in revelry and drunkenness, not in lewdness and lust, not in strife and envy. But put on the Lord Jesus Christ, and make no provision for the flesh, to fulfill its lusts.* (NKJV)

I would like to suggest that when we wrap ourselves in the tallit, we are symbolically putting on the Lord Jesus Christ, for He is our covering and righteousness. Could it also represent the light of the Lord, just as the Orthodox Jewish rabbis talk about the transcendent light that permeates creation, which one should emanate as the light of God in every sphere of Life and living? Jesus declared in John 8:12,

I am the light of the world. He who follows Me shall not walk in darkness, but have the light of life. (NKJV)

And consider this description of God in Hebrews 1:1–3:

God, who at various times and in various ways spoke in time past to the fathers by the prophets, has in these last days spoken to us by His Son, whom He has appointed heir of all things, through whom also He made the worlds; who being the brightness of His glory and the express image of His person, and upholding all things by the word of His power, when He had by Himself purged our sins, sat down at the right hand of the Majesty on high... (NKJV)

Notice that the Word describes Ye'Shua as *"the brightness of His glory and the express image of his person."* In other words, Ye'Shua is clothed in light, the very glory of God. Wow!

There is a deep spiritual significance that goes beyond the natural when one wraps himself in the tallit with the tzitzit and prays.

Our final consideration is the picture of Ruth asking Boaz to symbolically cover her under his wing. In the literal application, she was lying at his feet when he awoke, and she desired that he cover her under the border of his garment, which had the tassels attached. This was a declaration that she desired for him to cover her as her husband.

The application could not be clearer: Ruth was a Gentile who had come to Israel and sought out Boaz, the kinsman redeemer. Boaz is the type of Ye'shua the heavenly Bridegroom, the one to whom the church is betrothed. To wrap oneself in the tzitzit is to declare, prophetically, "I am betrothed to Christ the Messiah. I am His and He is mine." What an amazing picture of our intimacy with the Lord! Praise Adonai!

In conclusion, the wonderful truth is that under the tzitzit, the wings of the Lord, you will find healing according to the prophet Malichi. You will find refuge and protection according to the psalmist—and the covering of authority according to the book of Ruth.

The Shofar and Prayer

I would like to address the usage of shofars and their significance in prayer.

There are a number of reasons for the blowing of the shofars at designated occasions, but my focus very simply is to encourage you to recognize that the blowing of the shofar in intercessory prayer, under the leading of the Holy Spirit, can be a powerful tool of prayer.

We have a precedence in Scripture implying that the shofar is a weapon of war. The story of Gideon, in the book of Judges, reveals this truth. The Midianites had been oppressing Israel for a long time. God chose a reluctant Gideon, who needed a number of signs to be fulfilled by the angel before He agreed to lead Israel in battle. Finally, through the process of God, Gideon led an army of three hundred men and defeated the Midianites supernaturally. Let's look at the story in Judges 7:16–23:

> Then he divided the three hundred men into three companies, and he put a trumpet into every man's hand, with empty pitchers, and torches inside the pitchers. And he said to them, "Look at me and do likewise; watch, and when I come to the edge of the camp you shall do as I do: When I blow the trumpet, I and all who are with me, then you also blow the trumpets on every side of the whole camp, and say, 'The sword of the Lord and of Gideon!'"
>
> So Gideon and the hundred men who were with him came to the outpost of the camp at the beginning of the middle watch, just as they had posted the watch; and they blew the trumpets and broke the pitchers that were in their hands. Then the three companies blew the trumpets and broke the pitchers—they held the torches in their left hands and the trumpets in their right hands for blowing—and they cried, "The sword of the Lord and of Gideon!" And every man stood in his place all around the camp; and the whole army ran and cried out and fled. When the three hundred blew

the trumpets, the Lord set every man's sword against his companion throughout the whole camp; and the army fled to Beth Acacia, toward Zererah, as far as the border of Abel Meholah, by Tabbath.

And the men of Israel gathered together from Naphtali, Asher, and all Manasseh, and pursued the Midianites. (NKJV)

Look what happened when the shofars were blown and the pitchers were smashed: the enemy, which outnumbered the Israelites a hundred to one, went into confusion and fear and turned on each other. It was a supernatural victory that could not be explained physically.

I would suggest to you that our enemy, the kingdom of darkness, hates the sound of the shofar, especially when it is blown as a declaration of the victory of God over Satan or the kingdom of light over the kingdom of darkness. I personally believe that when the shofar is blown, under the leading of the Holy Spirit in prayer, the demonic powers and principalities go into confusion and fear. I have witnessed such oppressive atmospheres in prayer meetings, and they were dispelled; the moment we blew the shofars, we experienced a breakthrough!

Another pertinent example of the power of the shofar is the conquest of the city of Jericho. Once again, the Israelites experienced a supernatural victory by blowing the shofars under the instructions of the Lord—and the walls came down!

So the people shouted when the priests blew the trumpets. And it happened when the people heard the sound of the trumpet, and the people shouted with a great shout, that the wall fell down flat. Then the people went up into the city, every man straight before him, and they took the city. (Joshua 6:20, NKJV)

When we sound the shofar under the leading of the Ruach Ha Kodesh (the Holy Spirit) at specific times, the walls of opposition, and warfare in people's lives, come crashing down, and great victories are experienced in prayer.

I want to encourage you in your personal prayer times to sound the shofar, declaring the victory of the Lord over your situation. For pastors who are leading corporate prayer meetings, don't be afraid to sound the shofars when you need a breakthrough. I can assure you that it works and that our God is God; no demonic power or principality will be able to resist you when you blow that shofar in victory.

A final thought: the physical shofar, when it is first made, exudes an unpleasant smell because of the blood and marrow that was removed before it was formed. Interestingly, the more one blows the shofar, the quicker the smell dissipates and leaves. The symbolism is wonderful, as the shofar represents our life: the more we allow the Spirit of the Lord to blow through our lives, yielding to His work of shaping us into the image of Ye'Shua, the more the stench of fleshly pride, lust, and selfishness leaves our lives.

The shofar can also represent the refining work of the

Holy Spirit. For example, there are a variety of shofars, some partially refined and polished and others completely sanded down and polished. The point, very simply, is that we are all at different stages of sanctification in our lives, and the more we allow the Holy Spirit to smooth out the rough edges in our character, the more our lives will be conformed to the image of Christ.

The shofar is a wonderful visual that can be very helpful in your life of prayer.

14

Geopolitical Israel and the Church

WE HAVE CONSIDERED THE IMPORTANCE AND RELEVANCE of observing and celebrating the biblical feasts and understanding the Jewish roots of the faith in a Gentile context. There remains one final topic we must address to give us a complete picture of God's ultimate plan of redemption and restoration of all things.

Earlier in this book, I presented very clearly that the formation of the one new man pictured by the Apostle Paul in Ephesians 2–3 is the coming together of the Jew and Gentile believers, fulfilling the ultimate plan of God. Our understanding of this begins with the twentieth-century miracle of the establishment of the Jewish State of Israel. We cannot proceed forward if we do not recognize that the birth of the State of Israel in 1948 was a fulfillment of prophecy. Adding to this principle, we must acknowledge that the Jewish people have been specifically singled out by God to fulfill eternal purposes.

I believe we need to consider what God said to the people in the desert just prior to revealing His Torah on the mountains of Sinai, having delivered them from the slavery of the Egyptians.

Jacob's family, through Joseph, was spared annihilation by God's supernatural favor by saving them to Egypt. In Genesis 46:2–4, God speaks to Jacob hundreds of years earlier, in a vision at night, and says,

> *Then God spoke to Israel in the visions of the night, and said, "Jacob, Jacob!"*
> *And he said, "Here I am."*
> *So He said, "I am God, the God of your father; do not fear to go down to Egypt, for I will make of you a great nation there. I will go down with you to Egypt, and I will also surely bring you up again; and Joseph will put his hand on your eyes."* (NKJV)

The Bible then says that Jacob left Be'er-Sheva with his entire family and flocks and arrived in Egypt. Genesis 46:27 says, *"All the persons of the house of Jacob who went to Egypt were seventy"* (NKJV).

Consider closely the plan of God in sparing a family to create a nation in years to come—four hundred years later, in fact—leaving Egypt numbering in the millions. The purpose of God was to establish a nation that would be set apart for Him. Now consider what God said through Moses to the people of Israel just prior to giving them the Decalogue, the Ten Commandments:

And Moses went up to God, and the Lord called to him from the mountain, saying, "Thus you shall say to the house of Jacob, and tell the children of Israel: 'You have seen what I did to the Egyptians, and how I bore you on eagles' wings and brought you to Myself. Now therefore, if you will indeed obey My voice and keep My covenant, then you shall be a special treasure to Me above all people; for all the earth is Mine. And you shall be to Me a kingdom of priests and a holy nation.' These are the words which you shall speak to the children of Israel." (Exodus 19:3–6, NKJV)

It is clear that God has called the descendants of Abraham Isaac, and now specifically Jacob, *"a special treasure to Me above all people."* And secondly, *"a kingdom of priests and a holy nation."*

These descriptions of Israel, I believe, are the very reason for the intense antisemitism that through human time has reared its ugly head. This hatred and bitterness against the Jewish people is fueled by jealousy. The phrase "the chosen people" implies that God chose one nation and not the other nations. Immediately this evokes a response of rejection and hurt by those who were not chosen. It is human to feel excluded and passed over.

The conflict arises because many Gentiles have not understood that the choice was not made on the basis of worth and value. The distinction God makes is not qualitative but functional: *"And you will be to Me a kingdom of priests."*

The calling upon the Jewish people is a spiritual calling to carry the light of God into a world of moral darkness and confusion. The treasure of God is the light of His Word and glory, and it alone can dispel the darkness of sin, death, and destruction, bringing a restoration to all creation.

Suffice to say that Israel has not succeeded in fulfilling its assignment to be a light to the Gentile nations. The Apostle Paul picks up this argument in Romans 9:3–6:

> *For I could wish that I myself were accursed from Christ for my brethren, my countrymen according to the flesh, who are Israelites, to whom pertain the adoption, the glory, the covenants, the giving of the law, the service of God, and the promises; of whom are the fathers and from whom, according to the flesh, Christ came, who is over all, the eternally blessed God. Amen. But it is not that the word of God has taken no effect. For they are not all Israel who are of Israel...* (NKJV)

Please notice the wording that the Apostle Paul uses to describe his broken heart for the Jewish people of Israel. He describes the high calling and privilege that was given to Israel as *"the covenants, the giving of the law, the service of God, and the promises."* This describes the very lineage of the Messiah! Yet their present condition was discouraging; they were lost without a knowledge of the Messiah, Ye'shua. This was heavy on the apostle's heart, even though he had made it clear that his calling was to the Gentiles. Yes, Israel had failed in being a light to the Gentiles, but their failure did not result in a rejection of their election!

This is the key point that separates the Christian world into two camps: those who view Israel's failure as the reason for replacement theology, and those who see their failure as the outworking and emergence of the one new man of Ephesians 2–3.

I believe the New Testament makes it very clear that the inauguration of the church in Acts 2 was not a rejection of Israel by God, but in fact a fulfillment of prophecy and the indicator that this world had entered the season of the end times. It would seem to me that we need to differentiate the timeframe that the Scriptures refer to as the end-times and the end of days. Some scholars and teachers would declare that these terms mean the same thing, but I am going to seek to prove to you in the context of Scripture that there is a difference.

Acharit Hayamim = End-Times

In the Hebrew, according to the prophet Daniel, who was given visions and encounters regarding world history, the Archangel Gavri'el, coming in response to Daniel's prayer and fasting, declared to Him, *"So I have come to make you understand what will happen to your people [Israel] in the acharit-hayamim; for there is still another vision which will relate to those days"* (Daniel 10:14, CJB). The term *acharit-hayamim* is translated in the NKJV as the latter days, or end-times.

Olam Hazeh = End of Days

Then Jesus went out and departed from the temple, and His disciples came up to show Him the buildings of the temple. And Jesus said to them, "Do you not see all these things? Assuredly, I say to you, not one stone shall be left here upon another, that shall not be thrown down."

Now as He sat on the Mount of Olives, the disciples came to Him privately, saying, "Tell us, when will these things be? And what will be the sign of Your coming, and of the end of the age [olam hazeh]?"

And Jesus answered and said to them: "Take heed that no one deceives you. For many will come in My name, saying, 'I am the Christ,' and will deceive many. And you will hear of wars and rumors of wars. See that you are not troubled; for all these things must come to pass, but the end is not yet. For nation will rise against nation, and kingdom against kingdom. And there will be famines, pestilences, and earthquakes in various places. All these are the beginning of sorrows. (Matthew 24:1–8, NKJV)

Now consider another term used—or better yet, an expression that the disciples used in a question to Ye'shua. Just prior to this, they were on the Mount of Olives viewing the Temple Mount and the Eastern Gate (or as it was known, the Golden Gate). They were commenting on the beauty of the temple when Ye'shua shocked them by declaring that not one stone would be left upon another and the temple would be utterly destroyed. According to history, the Romans under General Titus crushed the Jewish rebellion and destroyed Yerushalayim and the temple, and thus they were the cause of the Jewish Diaspora that lasted until 1948.

In Matthew's Gospel, which we can safely say was written with a Jewish readership in mind, Jesus was clearly asked by His disciples when the fulfillment of the temple's destruction would take place:

> *When he was sitting on the Mount of Olives, the talmidim came to him privately. "Tell us," they said, "when will these things happen? And what will be the sign that you are coming, and that the 'olam hazeh is ending?"* (Matthew 24:3, CJB)

Notice that they asked three specific questions:
- When will these things happen? When will the temple be destroyed?
- What will be the sign of your coming?
- When will the *olam hazeh* end? When will this present world come to an end?

Jesus then begins to answer these questions, challenging them to be alert, watch out, and not let anyone fool them. You can read the entire chapter and study in detail some of the signs Jesus revealed regarding His return and the end of the world, but for the purposes of this writing, I want to draw your attention to the term olam hazeh (this present world). I believe these two expressions—the *acharit-hayamin* and the *olam hazeh*—convey separate meanings. The *acharit-hayamim* speaks of a season, or a dispensational timeframe, whereas the *olam hazeh* speaks of a definitive time—a conclusion, a termination of sorts.

Allow me to piece this together in an informed way, bringing clarity and revelation. The Old Testament prophets always prophesied in terms of geopolitical Israel and the surrounding nations. When they prophesied about the *acharit-hayamim*, they understood it to refer to the last phase of human history, the final season of God's dealing with the nations and their relationship to Israel. Therefore, we can safely say that since the establishment of the modern State of Israel, a twenty-first-century miracle, we have entered the season of the last days, the *acharit-hayamim*.

Geopolitical Israel is God's time-clock, the centerpiece of history and the unfolding of His final plan to rule and reign from Yerushalayim. The prophetic book of Joel gives us a glimpse of what will occur leading up to the termination of the *olam hazeh*:

> *For then, at that time, when I restore the fortunes of Y'hudah and Yerushalayim, I will gather all nations and bring them down to the Valley of Y'hoshafat [Adonai judges]. I will enter into judgment there for my people, my heritage Isra'el, whom they scattered among the nations; then they divided my land... "Let the nations be roused and come*

up to the Valley of Y'hoshafat [Adonai judges]. For there I will sit to judge all the surrounding nations." Swing the sickle, for the harvest is ripe; come, and tread, for the winepress is full. The vats are overflowing, for their wickedness is great. Such enormous crowds in the Valley of Decision! For the Day of Adonai is upon us in the Valley of Decision! The sun and moon have grown black, and the stars have stopped shining. Adonai will roar from Tziyon, he will thunder from Yerushalayim, the sky and the earth will shake. But Adonai will be a refuge for his people, a stronghold for the people of Isra'el. "You will know that I am Adonai your God, living on Tziyon my holy mountain." Then Yerushalayim will be holy, and foreigners will pass through her no more. Then, when that time comes, the mountains will drip with sweet wine, the hills will flow with milk, all the streambeds of Y'hudah will run with water, and a spring will flow from the house of Adonai to water the Sheetim Valley. But Egypt will be desolate and Edom a desert waste, because of the violence done to the people of Y'hudah, because they shed innocent blood in their land. Y'hudah will be inhabited forever, Yerushalayim through all generations. "I will cleanse them of bloodguilt which I have not yet cleansed," for Adonai is living in Tziyon. (Joel 4:1–2, 12–21, CJB)

Notice the powerful imagery to describe the judgment of God as the nations will be drawn to the Valley of Y'hoshafat, and God says that He will sit to judge the nations.

Read Joel 3:13 again: *"Swing the sickle, for the harvest is ripe; come, and tread, for the winepress is full. The vats are overflowing, for their wickedness is great"* (CJB). The picture of swinging the sickle refers to the fullness of judgment and the wickedness of the nations around Israel. The vats are full—referring to their sins and atrocities against God's people—and have reached their maximum effect. Sin has gone beyond what is permissible and tolerant, and the time is up. God will arise and destroy those wicked nations for all they have done to the Jewish people.

The tense language is just a glimpse of what it will look like when God's judgment is in full manifestation. This will then signal the ending of the *olam hazeh*, this present world, for the Lord Himself will rule and reign from Yerushalayim living on Tziyon, His holy mountain.

Now, there are a number of unanswered questions regarding the timeline of these events, but let me remind you that I believe the Holy Spirit strategically did not spell it out clearly because only those who study and search for the truth will have an idea of where we are at. The scoffers and skeptics will continue to rant and rave, but will be lost in eternity because of their unbelief. Those who love the Lord and His Word will be watching and waiting, living with expectation of Ye'shua's return and the fulfillment of all things.

Geopolitical Israel plays a vital role in the fulfillment of all things. If you were to exclude Israel's role and importance by declaring that the church has replaced her, you would have to remove large portions of God's Word to make that theology fit. I remind you that the Old Testament prophets neither saw nor prophesied the existence of the church. The Apostle Paul said it clearly in Ephesians 3:5–6:

> *...which in other ages was not made known to the sons of men, as it has now been revealed by the Spirit to His holy apostles and prophets: that the Gentiles should be fellow heirs, of the same body, and partakers of His promise in Christ through the gospel...* (NKJV)

You cannot get any clearer than that. Every prophecy spoken by the prophets, and Ye'shua Himself, regarding geopolitical Israel deals with the physical interpretation and existence of a nation. To deny this fact is to question and disqualify the authenticity of the Scriptures. If that is the case, then our faith and doctrinal positions are useless and vain. I believe that the church must recognize that the fulfillment of all things requires a strong relationship with the physical descendants of Abraham, Isaac, and Jacob; without their fullness, biblical prophecy cannot be fulfilled.

Supporting a Strong Advocacy for the State of Israel

In the context of this discussion, I believe it is very important to address why the Christian church should support and embrace a strong advocacy for the State of Israel. This is a valid question that deserves an answer from the Scriptures.

Most ardent supporters of Israel will declare that the reason for supporting Israel is the promise of blessing for those who bless Abraham's family according to Genesis 12:3: *"I will bless those who bless you, and I will curse him who curses you; and in you all the families of the earth shall be blessed"* (NKJV). This is definitely a good reason for a strong advocacy for Israel. But if you look at this a little more closely, this reason has an undertone of selfishness: "I want to be blessed, so I'd better bless Israel, or else I will forfeit this privilege!" I believe there is a more valid and significant reason, and God Himself gives us the reason very clearly in Ezekiel 39:21–29. Let's take a look:

I will set My glory among the nations; all the nations shall see My judgment which I have executed, and My hand which I have laid on them. So the house of Israel shall know that I am the Lord their God from that day forward. The Gentiles shall know that the house of Israel went into captivity for their iniquity; because they were unfaithful to Me, therefore I hid My face from them. I gave them into the hand of their enemies, and they all fell by the sword. According to their uncleanness and according to their transgressions I have dealt with them, and hidden My face from them.

Therefore thus says the Lord God: "Now I will bring back the captives of Jacob, and have mercy on the whole house of Israel; and I will be jealous for My holy name—after they have borne their shame, and all their unfaithfulness in which they were unfaithful to Me, when they dwelt safely in their own land and no one made them afraid. When I have brought them back from the peoples and gathered them out of their enemies' lands, and I am hallowed in them in the sight of many nations, then they shall know that I am the Lord their God, who sent them into captivity among the nations, but also brought them back to their land, and left none of them captive any longer. And I will not hide My face from them anymore; for I shall have poured out My Spirit on the house of Israel," says the Lord God. (NKJV)

This is the very reason for a strong advocacy of Israel: the Lord's name will be hallowed or honored in the sight of many nations. In Ezekiel 39:25 we find the key reason, as God declares, *"Now I will bring back the captives of Jacob, and have mercy on the whole house of Israel; and I will be jealous for My holy name..."* (NKJV)

When the Gentile church supports and embraces the State of Israel, the name of the Lord is honored and the Word of God affirmed among the nations. It's that straightforward! God loves the land and the Jewish people even though their sin and turning away from righteousness resulted in the Diaspora. Yet God says that He's bringing them back to the land for His name's sake!

Therefore, based on what God said through the prophet Ezekiel, to dismiss the importance of the modern twenty-first-century miracle of the establishment of the State of Israel is to make a costly mistake that will completely throw off-kilter one's understanding of Scripture, both exegetically and theologically. But most important of all, it makes light of what God thinks is important.

I would encourage every reader to reevaluate and reconsider their hearts regarding Israel and then make some adjustments if they presently do not align with God's heart for Israel.

Closing Thoughts

This concludes our journey of correlating biblical Judaism in a Gentile context. I challenge you to incorporate and seek to appropriate the principles and truths of the biblical feasts, for in their observance and practice will come a richness to your faith, increasing your revelation and relationship with God. To my Gentile readers, it is all for you to discover! Have the courage to step out of your religious box. You will never regret that decision, for you will truly come to know the Jewish Messiah, Ye'shua ha Mashiach, more intimately.

For my colleagues in the ministry, your responsibility to teach believers the entire counsel of God calls you to pursue with greater determination an understanding of biblical truth. Commit yourself to teaching the principles of the Jewish roots of faith, communicating them in a relevant and meaningful way, and I can assure you that your church will grow spiritually into a well-balanced and mature company of believers.

And may we say with clarity and conviction, "Next year in Yerushalayim!" This is the declaration of the Jewish people throughout history at the end of the Pesach Haggadah. May the Messiah come in our days, to His city, Jerusalem!

Appendix

THE FOLLOWING IS AN ESSAY I PRESENTED TO THE PARTICIPANTS of the Apostolic Prophet Convergence in Dallas, Texas, in December 2011 regarding the relationship between Israel and the church.

Relationship Between Israel and the Church (Ephesians 2:11–3:12)

In his apostolic letter to the Ephesian believers, the Apostle Paul clearly articulates God's ultimate plan of redemption and the culmination of all things. He presents his case by addressing the Gentile believers as the uncircumcised, foreigners, and strangers to the covenants of God and the nation of Israel without hope and without God. But now, through Jesus the Messiah, Gentile believers can become one with Israel, accessing the promises of the covenant, fulfilling the one new man plan of God, reconciling the Jew and Gentile believer back to the Father.

The end result of this union is clearly expressed in Ephesians 2:19: *"Now, therefore, you are no longer strangers and foreigners, but fellow citizens with the saints and members of the household of God"* (NKJV). This new DNA, the new humanity, is metaphorically compared to the house that God is building to showcase His glory. This house is built upon the foundation of the apostles and prophets with Ye'shua as the cornerstone.

Unpacking this more deeply, I believe that the apostolic and prophetic ministries are a functional representation of the one new man of God. Israel is the apostolic nation, having been set first according to the principle in 1 Corinthians 12:28: *"first apostles, second prophets, third teachers..."* (NKJV) Gentile believers who comprise the church reflect the prophetic element of God's plan birthed through the outpouring of the Holy Spirit. Earlier in this same chapter, we read,

> *For by one Spirit we were all baptized into one body— whether Jews or Greeks, whether slaves or free—and have all been made to drink into one Spirit.* (1 Corinthians 12:13, NKJV)

The parallel is unmistakable: Israel (the Jews) are apostolic, and the church (Gentile believers) are the prophetic, together forming the solid foundation. And Ye'shua is the cohesive cornerstone, holding the entire plan (building, house, family) together.

For clarity's sake, the cornerstone in Roman architecture was not the corner of two adjoining walls determining the coordinates and measurements of the house; it was the central stone in the structural design of the arches. Removal of the central stone from the arch would cause a collapse. The language and imagery is powerful, displaying the strategic plan of God and its fulfillment.

The apostle identifies God's ultimate strategy as a secret plan, a mystery

> ...and to make all see what is the fellowship of the mystery, which from the beginning of the ages has been hidden in God who created all things through Jesus Christ; to the intent that now the manifold wisdom of God might be made known by the church to the principalities and powers in the heavenly places, according to the eternal purpose which He accomplished in Christ Jesus our Lord... (Ephesians 3:9–11, NKJV)

A prime responsibility of the apostolic and prophetic ministry is to reveal and articulate the ultimate plan of God. Consider this:

> ...which in other ages was not made known to the sons of men, as it has now been revealed by the Spirit to His holy apostles and prophets: that the Gentiles should be fellow heirs, of the same body, and partakers of His promise in Christ through the gospel... (Ephesians 3:5–6, NKJV)

Having established the scriptural basis, I can proceed to present a picture of what this relationship looks like. The State of Israel and the Jewish people have been the continual target of antisemitism, prejudice, and hatred. The Islamic world, coupled with the liberal movement and left-leaning media, vilify Israel incessantly and its right to exist. The United Nations has literally been hijacked by oil-rich Arab states that are trying to monopolize and manipulate the European Union, the United States, Russia, and Canada into voting in favor of indictments against Israel, claiming that Israel is an apartheid state, abusive occupiers of Palestinian lands.

Unfortunately, Israel is losing the propaganda war and the liberal media is inflicting continual blows. Long-standing alliances with Western nations are deteriorating, as one by one they capitulate and buckle under the pressure, distancing themselves from Israel. There is a growing consensus among the Jewish people that the stage is being set for a conflagration that will see Israel stand alone against its enemies, abandoned by its former allies, primarily the United States.

However, the Jewish people are increasingly noticing the evangelical, full gospel Christians arising to voice their support for the State of Israel. Centuries of distrust and fear between Christians and Jews is beginning to dissipate, spurred by initiatives that promote reconciliation, forgiveness, and a bond of love. The posture of Ruth-like churches declare, *"For wherever you go, I will go... Your people shall be my people, and your God, my God. Where you die, I will die..."* (NKJV) This is beginning to melt the hardest Jewish heart.

As Ruth clung to her Jewish mother-in-law and would not let go, the church must do the same to Israel. Only sacrificial, unconditional love can reach the people and cause them to recognize the Messiah. The Gentile church must provoke the Jewish people to jealousy as they observe the extravagant love that Gentile believers have for the God of Ereta-Yisra'el, the land and the people. This alone will cause the dry, disillusioned, and discouraged Jewish people, the Naomis, to once again recognize their heavenly Boaz as Ye'shua, the Messiah.

The final outcome is even more glorious. The fruit of Boaz's and Ruth's love was a son named Obed. Consider what Ruth 4:14–17 declares:

> *Then the women said to Naomi, "Blessed be the Lord, who has not left you this day without a close relative; and may his name be famous in Israel! And may he be to you a restorer of life and a nourisher of your old age; for your daughter-in-law, who loves you, who is better to you than seven sons, has borne him." Then Naomi took the child and laid him on her bosom, and became a nurse to him. Also the neighbor women gave him a name, saying, "There is a son born to Naomi." And they called his name Obed. He is the father of Jesse, the father of David.* (NKJV)

As the church blesses, loves, and pursues the Jewish people when governments and nations abandon them, this extravagant love will birth a relationship that will supernaturally cause the Jewish people to recognize their redeemer and lactate again. Spiritual life will begin to flow from Israel and the light of God's Word will go forth from Zion, fulfilling the eschatological promise proclaimed in Isaiah 2:2–3:

> *Now it shall come to pass in the latter days tThat the mountain of the Lord's house shall be established on the top of the mountains, and shall be exalted above the hills; and all nations shall flow to it. Many people shall come and say, "Come, and let us go up to the mountain of the Lord, to the house of the God of Jacob; He will teach us His ways, and we shall walk in His paths." For out of Zion shall go forth the law, and the word of the Lord from Jerusalem.* (NKJV)

About the Author

REVEREND GIULIO LOREFICE GABELI IS THE NATIONAL DIRECTOR of the Canada Celebrates Israel Network of Christians and Jews, and the Canadian Liaison of the Knesset Christian Allies Caucus, affiliated with the Israel Allies Foundation, dedicated to promoting friendship and cooperation with political governments, as well as facilitating dialogue between Christian and Jewish organizations with the State of Israel. He is committed to pursuing the establishment of the "one new man" comprised of Jew and Gentile believers according to what is recorded in Ephesians 2–3. As the church takes her place to stand with Israel, he believes this will fulfill the ultimate plan of God and the culmination of all things.

Rev. Gabeli also serves as the Director of the Hope Vancouver Network and is the Chair of Voices Together Vancouver, which serves the Association of Christian Ministries of Greater Vancouver. He serves as well as an overseer of the Canadian Assemblies of God and is an advisor to a number of national Canadian ministries. He is the senior pastor of Westwood Community Church in Vancouver, a multicultural congregation with a number of ethnic satellite works.

He ministers along with his spouse of thirty-one years, Lina, an ordained full-time minister as well, and is the father of four children and a granddaughter. He resides in Vancouver, British Columbia, Canada.